To Tony, *compadre y compañero*

Contents

Foreword by Jack Miffleton   vii

Prologue   xv

PART I
A Travel Bag of Surprises

Chapter One: Preparing to Flee   3

Chapter Two: European Whirlwind, 1969   9

Chapter Three: A Taste of Mother England   19

Chapter Four: Paris Revisited   27

Chapter Five: Nightmare at De Gaulle   31

Chapter Six: Students in Israel   35

Chapter Seven: Greco-Austro-Hungarian Interlude   47

Chapter Eight: A Family Album in Spain   53

Chapter Nine: More Snapshots of Spain   59

Chapter Ten: Surveying Seville and Surroundings   69

PART II
Adventures in the "New World"

Chapter Eleven: California Nuggets   75

Chapter Twelve: Hawaiian Highlights   81

Chapter Thirteen: Capital Capers   85

Chapter Fourteen: To Mexico with Love   91

Two Padres on Holiday

My Travels with Tony

A Memoir

By

E. D. Osuna

aventine press

Published by Aventine Press
55 E. Emerson St.
Chula Vista, CA 91911
www.aventinepress.com

ISBN: 978-1-59330-969-5

Library of Congress Control Number: 2019918652
Library of Congress Cataloging-in-Publication Data
Memoir/E. D. Osuna

Printed in the United States of America

PART III
Blending the New and the Ageless

Chapter Fifteen: Manhattan Prelude   103

Chapter Sixteen: Italy From Tip to Toe   107

Chapter Seventeen: Slices of Sicily   113

Chapter Eighteen: Roman Reprise   117

Chapter Nineteen: Manhattan Encore   123

Chapter Twenty: All Aboard for Russia   127

PART IV
Sites of Grace and Insight

Chapter Twenty-One: Shameless Pilgrims on El Camino 135

Chapter Twenty-Two: Egyptian Escapade   139

Chapter Twenty-Three: Mary's House   141

Chapter Twenty-Four: *Semana Santa en Sevilla*   143

Chapter Twenty-Five: A Pilgrim's Pageant   149

Epilogue   153

Acknowledgments   155

Addendum: A Toast to Father Antonio A. Valdivia   157

Cover design and photo-art by Jerry A. Rubino

FOREWORD

For over forty years Don Osuna has been a treasured friend of mine. He is celebrated in the Diocese of Oakland as a musician, former rector of the Oakland Cathedral, successful pastor and a creative presence, especially during the decades following the Second Vatican Council. In retirement he still continues a pastoral ministry.

Don's creativity has emerged again in this, his latest book, where he shares memories comprising fifty years of travel experiences with his good friend, classmate and fellow priest, Tony Valdivia. As in Kerouac's classic *On the Road* and Steinbeck's evocative search for America in *Travels with Charlie*, Don uses a travelogue format to explore the values of friendship, leisure, travel and play. Over the years I have heard some of these wonderful stories at dinners and other occasions. It is a delight to see them in print.

I invite you, dear reader, to find what I have found in these memories – a picture of friendship bonded by travel adventures, humor, music, culture and even the inevitable exhaustion that can accompany travel. With Don as my guide I will reflect on the significance to me of his memories and the merits of travel, leisure and play in human life.

Travel
Mark Twain in his book, *Innocents Abroad*, observes that travel is fatal to prejudice, bigotry, and narrow-

mindedness. For most of us, travel has a way of enriching our lives and making us grow as human beings. It was once the privilege of the wealthy and educated, but today advances in transportation have opened the world to pilgrims from everywhere. For many fortunate students foreign travel is what caps a liberal arts or classical education.

I recall my first visit to Rome as a graduate student where I discovered a manhole cover engraved with SPQR – the ancient emblem of the Roman republic *Senatus Populusque Romanus* meaning the "Senate and Roman People." I congratulated myself for staying awake during that lecture in ancient history. I also remember a trip to Budapest with my Hungarian-born wife. We visited one of Budapest's many museums, and the captions by the exhibits were in Hungarian and Latin. My wife asked, "Shall I translate the Hungarian for you?" I replied, "No need, this is one of the few times that my many years of Latin will be helpful!" Leaving the museum, I felt better about my rather impractical education. Of course, education is a life-long process, and travel above all else reinforces an understanding of history, language, literature, art, geography and most of all, human diversity.

Don's stories of his first visits with Tony to France, Germany and Italy are engaging, colorful and obviously reside in a very happy place in Don's mind. Both Tony and Don have linguistic talents with little fear of venturing into a foreign language on the fly. His stories of grappling with the many contexts for using the German word, *Bitte,* and in trying to ask for the check in a French restaurant are hilarious and relatable.

Don leads a culinary journey not only around Paris but in Spain, including, of course, homemade paella and lots of Rioja. To be in Israel for Palm Sunday and to celebrate an Orthodox Holy Week would be a treat for any Catholic, but to experience the Easter mysteries with commentary by Don and Tony brings both humor and insight into the gospels as they follow the footsteps of Jesus.

As anyone who flies to foreign countries knows, airports can be tedious, and flight connections can often be met with delays, also bad weather and unreliable ground transportation can disrupt one's travels, and as Don remembers danger lurks even from international conflicts. But Don does not avoid writing about these hassles because with Tony's humor, peaceful demeanor and joy (*Paz y Alegría*) they always seem to recover with aplomb and travel on! Yes, travel can keep one off balance, but in the end, it is the ultimate education as St. Augustine wrote: "The world is a book, and those who do not travel read only a page."

Leisure
One has often heard the phrase "an idle mind or even an idle man is the devil's workshop." While this is not a literal translation from the Book of Proverbs, it is accepted as an aphorism in some cultures. But leisure is different

from laziness. There is also the famous saying that all work and no play make Jack a dull boy. Without leisure would music, art, literature or philosophy exist?

Josef Pieper, a modern scholastic philosopher, wrote what is now a classic treatise, *Leisure: The Basis of Culture,* reclaiming our human dignity in a culture of workaholism.

Pieper maintains that leisure is not the same as the absence of activity. The greatest art, the most engaging concepts in philosophy, the spark for every technological advancement originated in leisure, in those moments of quiet contemplation. He believes that living in a commodity-oriented world has caused many people to mistake making a living with having a life. Pieper further points out that the origin of the Latin word *scola* (school) is from the Greek word for leisure. Schools were once intended as places of leisure and contemplative activity. Pieper writes that the original meaning of the concept of leisure has nearly been forgotten in today's overemphasis on the world of work.

As with diet or good health, it is usually a matter of balance. Leisure is not at war with work, but various cultures do balance the two differently. As a young man I had the opportunity to live in Italy for over a year in a small town outside of Rome. Many days of the week I would take the bus into Rome. At least two or three times a month my bus, though behind schedule, was parked at my stop with the driver standing outside, chatting and smoking with passengers. The first time it happened I asked the driver, "Is there some mechanical problem?" "No Signore," he replied, "It's a *sciopero*," (a strike!) "But only for one hour today, and one hour tomorrow," he added. I continued, "Are you striking for better wages or benefits?" "Oh no, Signore," he replied, "We want a four-day workweek."

As with travel, leisure has historically been the privilege of the upper-class. Opportunities for leisure multiplied as the middle classes gained more wealth in the last century. But the use of leisure time is multivalent, and travel is only one of myriad possibilities. In this context I am only addressing how leisure has provided travel and vacation opportunities. A true vacation is one set loose from work-time, creating a freedom, a root sense of "holi-day," a time of "holi-ness," a sacred pause.

Play
Beginning in 1959, the General Assembly of the United Nations found it very important to write declarations protecting the world's children and supporting their right to play and leisure. As a music teacher for over thirty years in an elementary school, I know quite a bit about play and how young children learn from play. First of all, play is enjoyable, it is spontaneous, it engages one actively and it has an element of make believe. It does not surprise me to find all of these childlike ingredients present in Don's memoir. He even refers to his travels as playtime!

The word "play" is ubiquitous in the English language and probably evolved from an Anglo-Saxon word for movement, exercise or dance. When my wife was learning English, she would complain: "That word "play" has so many different meanings, it's confusing!" Play the piano, play chess, play the radio, play baseball, play with fire, etc. As a noun it can describe a maneuver in football or a theatrical performance. In this latter context play demonstrates one element of childhood fun that I mentioned above – "make-believe." Don recalls an amusing venture with Tony into the world of "make-believe." He and Tony were visiting a Georgetown nightclub and were told there were no tables available or even standing room. In front of the hostess Don pretended to be an interpreter, speaking to Tony in Spanish, then introducing him as the Ambassador of Venezuela. Of course, the story in Don's words contains much more drama, but the "ambassador" and his "interpreter" were seated! Play is not wasted time, but rather time spent building new knowledge from previous experience, and in Don's travels with Tony play is not just fun but useful!

In *A Theology of Play* the German theologian, Jürgen Moltmann, maintains that play and leisure are not useless activities, but foreshadow the joy of the final event in the divine plan! In play we can echo God's creative action for God did not create out of necessity, but because God is playful. Play, then can be seen as a spiritual activity because it rejuvenates and injects a spirit of bliss and joy into human life. According to Moltmann the future reality that God intended is revealed in moments of play. So, in this theology, play that begins in nursery school actually anticipates the Parousia!

Memory

Don Osuna has a remarkable memory for details that occurred during his travel decades ago. It is indeed good fortune to live long enough to write a memoir, but to be able to share that treasure house of the mind is truly amazing. It appears to me that the memories preserved in this work are not just the kind of memory that recalls what one had for dinner last night. Memories over time that build friendships are in a different category.

The Greek word *anamnesis* describes a Semitic understanding of memory not wholly contained in the English word "memory." Liturgists use this concept of memory to explain how in the Mass the Paschal Mystery is made present once again. I believe that this kind of remembering also enriches human relationships. I call it memory plus – plus love, trust and imagination. It is mythic memory, making the past present again. For example, when a young couple meet for a first date, perhaps with dinner and a movie, and then a few weeks later recall the details of the date, the memory is not very deep in mythic meaning. But when they remember that first meeting after forty years of marriage and life together with its ups and downs, joys and sorrows, it is a deeper, richer remembering. Forty years of living and dying are now brought to bear on the original memory, and what it will be when this couple lie down to die and what it makes of them all their days until then, that is the real memory, a blest memory.

Finally, dear reader, I invite you again to find what I have found in this memoir – a portrait of friendship enriched by travel adventures, humor, music and culture; the unique story of two friends collecting blest memories that have given shape and quality to their lives.

Jack Miffleton

Both the author and his classmate Antonio "Tony" A. Valdivia are priests of the Diocese of Oakland in California. Currently they are retired but continue to be active in parish ministry. E. D. (Donald) Osuna is also the author of *"How Awesome is This Place!" (Genesis 28:17):* My Years at the Oakland Cathedral, 1967-1986.

Prologue

In my first memoir, I described my work. This one is about how I spent my playtime. In my diocese, priests are given a yearly one month's vacation plus a few days after Christmas and Easter. Every seven years or so one can request an extended sabbatical.

Over the past 50 years much of my holiday travel has been with my classmate Tony. It's been a lot of fun because Tony is easy going, fun loving, entertaining and a delightful companion. We've had a lot of enriching experiences as we covered much of the globe. If you're interested and have the time, buckle up, come along and join *Two Padres on Holiday.*

PART I

A Travel Bag of Surprises

Chapter One: Preparing to Flee

I'm driving the rental car. It's a task I would be given throughout our years of motoring together. Tony prefers the luxury of being chauffeured and the freedom of savoring the scenery.

We are on our way from Hartford, Connecticut, to Boston, Massachusetts. It is our first trip to the East Coast. Approaching the historic Bean Town coastline, Tony rolls down his window, leans his head into the wind, sniffs the air like an excited hound, and declares, "This must be a Catholic city. I smell sin!"

Spoken like a perceptive newly ordained confessor.

Tony's olfactory and visceral instincts surfaced again in Manhattan a couple of years later. We landed in New York City to visit my brother Jess, a stage and film actor who lived with his wife and toddler at Westbeth. The sprawling low-income complex is exclusively for practitioners of the fine arts. As we entered the lobby of the converted Con Edison building Tony's intuitive antennae popped up. Intently surveying the premises and breathing in the energy, he mused: "Can you imagine growing up surrounded by all these actors, writers, dancers and artists? All this creativity is bound to blow any kid's mind!"

From New York we were to fly to Europe. It was the fall of 1969, at the end of the devastating decade of the

1960's that witnessed the assassinations of John Kennedy, Martin Luther King Jr. and Robert Kennedy. Add to that, the Vietnam War, the Civil Rights Movement, the student uprisings, the Black Panther Party – the litany of upheavals goes on.

And not only in civil society. The Catholic Church, too, was in the throes of the reforms of the Second Vatican Council. As newly ordained priests we were thrown into the front lines of that revolution. By the end of the decade we had had enough of social and religious unrest. Hopefully, a tour of Europe would refresh our wearied spirits.

I remember the day we decided to flee the country. It was at La Barca, a popular Mexican cantina on Lombard Street in San Francisco. We used to go there on our day off or on a Saturday night after hearing confessions. Jose the bartender had found out that Tony and I used to sing Mexican songs together as seminarians. So, whenever we arrived he would hand me a guitar and Tony a pair of maracas. "The Singing Padres," he would announce, "will now entertain all you thirsty sinners with some *música ranchera*." As "repayment," freshly blended Margaritas would appear. However, since our hands were busy strumming and keeping rhythm and our lips mouthing lyrics, we rarely had time to consume the Tequila-laced concoctions.

One Wednesday evening, two fellow clerics showed up in the middle of our rendition of *Cucurrucucu Paloma*: a six-foot-four Roman-trained classmate and his "Very

Reverend" Vatican colleague. While we played and sang, the two Roman graduates freely helped themselves to our unclaimed Margaritas. We lost track of them – until closing time.

At 2 a.m. we hung up our instruments and exited the empty restaurant. But who do we find propped up on the hood of a parked Buick on Lombard Street but the future "Most Reverend" colleague? "Have you seen your classmate?" he asked, then added, "The last I saw him he was headed for the men's room. He didn't look so good."

We began banging on La Barca's shuttered doors. When they swung open, our six-foot-four classmate materialized, pale as a blended Margarita, trying to stabilize himself in the darkened threshold. Unable to locate or navigate his car, he ended up in ours. On the way over the Bay Bridge we overheard a groaning voice in the back seat mumbling a solemn vow, "I will never touch another one of those!"

The two of us in the front seat solemnly resolved to get out of town!

"The Singing Padres"

Chapter Two: European Whirlwind, 1969

Our first European escapade was a whirlwind tour of the continent. Three weeks were spent mostly on planes, trains, buses, taxis, aching feet or in hotel rooms, exhausted and drained. After packing and unpacking, we hardly had time to "savor the scenery" or even get a decent taste of the culture. Here are a few morsels and sips – from out of the whirlwind.

Germany

Cologne
Tony fancies himself a polyglot. He has a musical ear and a facility for picking up foreign phrases. He is fluent in Spanish and English; he holds his own in Latin, Italian and Portuguese. Throughout his ministry he's memorized words and sentences in Polish, French, Russian, Chinese, Vietnamese and German. He has no hesitation in approaching strangers and, regardless of their native tongue, engaging them in lively conversation.

We landed in the northern German city of Cologne. The first day we toured the port and climbed the 509 stone steps of the cathedral's fabled tower. Early the next morning we headed for the ferry terminal, boarded a large sightseeing ship and started down the Rhine River. Our intention was to take the eight-hour cruise to Mainz. However, an unforeseen miscalculation on my part changed our plans.

Tony, of course, employing his meager Teutonic vocabulary, immediately fell into a lively conversation with a group of

Franciscan nuns. I chose to look for a table in the main lounge to view the majestic castles and citadels along the stately riverbanks.

I did discover one thing about the German language. Native speakers use the word *bitte* to convey a variety of meanings. The first is "Please"; it can also mean "Pardon?" or "Sorry?" or just "Uh?" At any rate, it was the only German word I knew.

A solicitous waiter approached and uttered something unintelligible. I wasn't sure, but he seemed to be asking a question. So, I responded *Bitte*. I thought I was saying "Pardon?" He obviously took it as "Please." Before another castle floated by, the solicitous waiter was placing in front of me a bottle of Rhine Riesling and a large wineglass.

I must have repeated *Bitte* several times more because when Tony finally showed up, there were three empty bottles on the table. As many hours had gone by. There was no way I could stay on that floating barge in my condition. "I've got to get off this ship – now!" I insisted. "My head and my legs are swimming – as are all these castles," I cried. Tony responded, *Bitte?* "I'm seasick," I confessed, "I'm going to throw up all over this boat unless we get off – right now!"

We disembarked at the next stop. Firm land and a brisk walk to the train station restored my equilibrium and my reeling head. Waiting for the train that would take us into town, I turned to Tony and said, "The wine wore off." Having set his mind and ear to the polyglot position, he registered my observation as *daswineworeoff. Bitte?* he said. I retorted, "I'm speaking ENGLISH!"

Coblenz

Coblenz is an ancient city situated on both banks of the Rhine at its confluence with the Moselle. It is a picturesque tourist destination. Luckily we found a quaint hostel perched on a bluff overlooking the two rivers. From its kitchen floated mouth-watering aromas.

The owner suggested that we have dinner in the garden near the edge of the cliff. The evening was warm and there was a full moon. Below us glistening in the moonlight we could see the Rhine winding its way toward Mainz.

Tony and the waiter exchanged a few words about the menu. Soon he returned with a large tray, which he deposited in the middle of the table. On it was an enormous platter laden with lamb shanks garlanded with a mound of potatoes and carrots stewed in gravy that tasted like the essence of grape – a gift, we surmised, from Máni the Norse moon god! All that was missing was a soundtrack by the grandiose composer of German opera, Richard Wagner.

Munich

We did not have to wait long for that. In Munich we obtained tickets to *Der fliegende Hollander,* Wagner's "Flying Dutchman." It was to be our last night in Germany; the next morning we had reservations on an early flight to Florence. To make sure "nothing goes wrong," Tony secured our airplane tickets and passports in a briefcase which he carried with him to the recently rebuilt *Nationaltheater München,* home of the Bavarian State Opera.

I've noticed one thing about Tony: The perception of beauty or bombast invariably propels him into spasms of ecstasy. Whether it is driving across the Golden Gate Bridge, watching an epic movie or listening to monumental music, his focus intensifies, his imagination expands, his spirit sails, soars and swells into waves of bliss bordering on rapture.

Needless to say, he flipped out at Wagner's spectacular portrayal of the legendary ghost-ship captain doomed to travel endless seas until redeemed by the undying love of the hefty soprano sea-goddess. So carried away in fact, that Tony forgot all about the briefcase securely stuffed under his seat!

We were a block away from the opera house when he realized that he had left behind the only way we were going to reach our next destination. Without passports, we were as doomed as the hapless captain of the opera. *Bitte!*

We sprinted back to the darkened ticket office. A lone attendant was inside. Tony put on a performance worthy of a seasoned Wagnerian tenor. He started pounding on the doors, windows and anything else in sight. Gesticulating hysterically, he began belting out an aria of impending disaster. The shocked attendant froze in amazement as this crazed tourist wailed, *Morgen – ich fliegande Amerikaner!* Pointing to the emptied opera hall

Tony roared, *Mein passporte!* Then he went into a telling pantomime, flapping his arms like a bird about to take flight, dancing and prancing around in circles he mimicked a traveler bemoaning a lost suitcase, which, he made clear, was located under a chair – pointing once again to the empty hall– *innerhalb!*

A wave of recognition came over the attendant's face. He opened the door. *Bitte!* he blurted. To our grateful relief he escorted the distraught *Amerikaner* to his vacated seat. Once Tony retrieved the treasured briefcase, the bemused attendant led him to the front door. Then in a gracious gesture of appreciation for a memorable performance he applauded heartily and chanted, "*Bravo, bravissimo!*"

Italy

Florence
In Florence we were looking forward to seeing Michelangelo's statue of David. Stupidly, we had arrived at the Accademia Gallery without reservations. We queued up and stood in an endless line. When we finally got into the museum, the place was overflowing with spectators. There was no way to get anywhere near the statue standing on a low pedestal in the middle of the multitude. All we could see in the distance was the top of a marble torso lunging out of a sea of heads like a drowning giant surfacing for air.

Extremely disappointed, we headed for the exit. But the Italian Muses were looking out for us. Tacked on a bulletin board near the door was an announcement inviting the public to a piano concert that very evening. A local artist would be performing three sonatas by Ludwig van Beethoven.

At 7:30 we entered the same spacious hall. This time it was silent and welcoming. Rows of chairs encircled a nine-foot concert grand piano nestled at the feet of the David – gloriously aglow in a halo of spotlights. The initial vision was breathtaking. What ensued was transcendent - a priceless experience well worth the wait. For me, it was the highlight of the entire 3,000-mile trip!

For two hours our gaze was fixed on the stone figure of a defiant youth intent upon defeating a formidable opponent. Comfortably seated, we had time to study every inch of that fearless prince poised to hurtle his death-inflicting weapon at a menacing, invisible Goliath.

As if interpreting in sound what our eyes beheld, Beethoven's voice sang of brewing battles, calculated combats and climactic clashes. It was the voice of a combatant confronting inner demons and struggling with an inexorable foe that would render him deaf. But in the end the victim would be victorious and trumpet in triumph an Ode to Joy!

Looking at and listening to those two warriors was a memorable meditation and compelling commentary on human courage, determination, faith and ultimate conquest over adversity. Bravo, bravissimo!

San Remo

By the time we reached San Remo on the Italian Riviera I was hopelessly homesick. I was ready to catch the next flight westward. "If I don't see, hear or eat something American," I said to my equally nostalgic companion, "I'm out of here!" Tony, on the other hand, was determined to tough it out; he was not about to entertain changes in itinerary. "I haven't come 3,000 miles just to turn back after two weeks!" Changing the subject, he added, "You're right. It's time to get something to eat."

Tony recalls places we have visited not by name or location but by their cuisine. I remember the venues, he the menus. San Remo is a good example. We were walking along a cobblestone street in this quaint Mediterranean resort village when I heard the distinctive piano styling of Erroll Garner playing "Misty." The music was floating out of a small trattoria called "Joe's Bistro." *Jazz at last – and at an American establishment!*

Tony can tell you the exact preparation of the pizza and pasta. What I remember besides the music is the dessert and the after-dinner drink. Giuseppe "Mister Joe owner-chef" insisted that we taste the specialty of the house - his signature flan, an egg-based custard with caramelized syrup. It was baking in his pizza oven. Heavenly! But the kicker was the bottle of sparkling wine Mr. Joe ceremoniously uncorked: Asti Spumante, a bubbly brew, sweeter than champagne and just as feisty. The combination of American music and Italian cuisine dissolved any former fatigue and induced an incipient euphoria.

The meal at Joe's, however, was just the appetizer. What followed was a visual smorgasbord. Just down the street the local cinema was showing Fellini's latest epic. We innocently purchased two tickets. We had no idea that critics had labeled the film "either a celebration of depravity or a warning against godlessness." Our assessment of the "combustible celluloid"? A psychedelic romp through Roman scenarios. *Had we heard too many confessions to be shocked?* Our reaction? An adolescent fit of the giggles – no doubt induced by Mr. Joe's pizza, pasta, flan and bubbly.

San Remo was a complete emotional catharsis for two weary travelers, dispelling any need for premature departures. We spent the rest of the evening in spasms of laughter. Before we knew it – time to leave for Paris.

France

Paris

Of course, we didn't have time on this trip to do much. But, since this was the capital of high *couture*, "We should at least," Tony suggested, "get a haircut." So, we made an appointment at a nearby beauty salon. I was told that my hair was *trop sec*. I was given a special treatment with conditioners to replenish the oils that the Italian sun had depleted. Tony opted for "the works," which turned out to be a *bouffant* that included a shampoo, scissor cut, hair styling, contour shaping, blow-dry and hairspray. The end result was a spectacular pompadour!

Sporting our Parisian hairdos, we splurged and reserved a table at the Hotel George Cinq, one of Paris' most elegant and expensive restaurants. The cuisine, of course, was gourmet and the service impeccable. Then came time to pay for the extravagance. While in France I usually acted as spokesman since my French was a trifle better than my classmate's. I asked for "le cheque." The waiter registered a quizzical look. *la CONTE, s'il vous plait,* I rephrased. Complete incomprehension. Out of the corner of my eye I could see Tony mentally scrounging his computer brain for alternatives. Giving me a classic French condescending smile, he nonchalantly but triumphantly asserted, *l'addition.*

Ah, mais oui monsieur !

It was obvious the next day as we boarded the TWA aircraft for SFO that Tony had not gotten much sleep. He admitted it on the plane: He was too afraid of mussing his *coiffure!*

Everything fell back into place, including hairstyles, as we resumed our pastoral ministries. Exposure to so many different landscapes and cultures in such a short time had been overwhelming. At the same time, it whetted our appetite and provided an incentive for planning future excursions. Our prayer however was that they would be less hectic and include more intermingling with the "natives."

Evidently the Saints from Great Britain were listening.

Chapter Three: A Taste of Mother England

Cambridge

Father Gary, associate pastor of the Church of the British Martyrs in Cambridge, picked us up at Heathrow Airport. Sister Margaret, religious education director at the parish, was with him. On the way home, puzzled as to what route Father Gary was taking Sister asked: "Where are you going?" Gary responded, "It's a short cut." Delighted, Sister Margaret chirped, "How cunning!"

A couple of years earlier, Gary and his seminary classmate Michael had knocked on the door of the cathedral rectory in downtown Oakland, California. They identified themselves as two deacons from England looking for directions to St. Albert's Priory, a local Dominican monastery. "Are you Dominicans?" I asked. "No, we are diocesan seminarians on holiday. We're just looking for lodging." Since we too were diocesan clergy, I invited them to stay with us. "That would be brilliant! Thank you so much!"

The next morning, I found our British guests in the kitchen. "We are astonished," Gary confessed. "We were sitting here when His Grace came down and made his own breakfast!" "We call him 'Bishop,'" I clarified. "And yes, our cook comes only in the afternoon to prepare the evening meal." "The Bishop mentioned that you are the cathedral dean." "Here in the States I'm called rector." "How stunning!"

That afternoon I introduced our visitors to Tony. Always eager and ready to "foster vocations" – and have a good time in the process – he suggested that we expose our European visitors to some of California's scenic attractions. Lake Tahoe in the Sierra Nevada would be perfect.

The three-hour drive through Northern California's valleys and snow-crested peaks fascinated and charmed our young tourists. So did the gaming tables at the Nevada border, where we concluded our tour with dinner at the restaurant atop Harvey's Casino. Asked if the Englishmen would like something after dessert, the response was, "Shall we retire to the lounge and sip some brandy and have a cigar?"

Now, we found ourselves sharing brandy and cigars in Cambridge "athwart the River Cam" in the diocese of East Anglia, 65 miles north of London. As his first assignment, Gary had landed in the city's only Roman Catholic parish. It happened to be the home of John Major, the British prime minister who, we found out later, converted to Catholicism. *Did Gary have anything to do with that?* We wondered.

The university town is immaculately groomed, with rolling hills and sprawling lawns. But aside from academic halls and student pubs there wasn't much to do or see. "Sorry, no casinos here!" After a couple of days Gary and Michael arranged for Tony and me to take the train to London and stay at a hotel across from Buckingham Palace. Our gracious hosts dropped us off at the train station and bade us farewell - "Do have loads of fun!"

London

On the station's platform a few commuters were waiting for the daily to London. Among them, to our immense surprise, was one of our bishop's classmates, Father Matthew P. Sullivan. Bishop John had told us that Matt loved all things British. In fact, his hobby was researching and experiencing the country's history, culture and cuisine, and spending much of his vacation in England. He had even written a book on the subject!

It was a godsend for us and a delight for Matt; he could now share with two first-time visitors the wonders of his favorite sport. "Meet me at 5 o'clock at Inn in the Park," he said. "We'll have a drink at the lounge and then go to the Savoy for dinner."

The exclusive hotel Inn in the Park was a stroll away through legendary Hyde Park – hence the name. What impressed me more than the luxurious marbled lobby were the people in it: numerous Saudi Arabians in traditional headdress and flowing tunics. At the entrance a stretch limousine pulled up and disgorged several women in head-to-foot black burkas with eye slits; two of them wore silver beaks attached to their noses. They were hurriedly ushered to the elevators.

Inside, a swarm of Arabian officials were bowing to and heralding the appearance of their prince who was sailing down the grand marble staircase resplendent in regal robes of white. It reminded one of a flock of cardinals at a papal audience. It also recalled the ties that a former empire still retains with former colonial territories.

At the cocktail lounge Matt regaled us with the history of major sites in London: Canterbury, St. Paul's, the Tower, Buckingham Palace, Victoria Station, Piccadilly Circus – all of which we would visit in time. For now, Matt would lead us to the Savoy Hotel on the Strand in the City of Westminster in central London.

Entering the Savoy Grill off the Strand was like being transported into the Victorian era. The maitre d' recognized Father Matthew as a regular patron and seated us at a favored table. A captain and a bevy of waiters catered to every need and desire. Tony will never forget the roast beef prepared in traditional British fashion. When it was time for the entrée, a chef in full regalia wheeled over a carving table with a huge platter covered with a silver dome. With a flourish he removed the shining lid. There in Elizabethan splendor lay an entire prime rib roast.

"What is the gentleman's desire?" asked the chef. The protocol was for the gentleman to point to his selection of cut, or indicate verbally which portion the master carver was to slice and serve. Matt noted Tony's flustered reaction and politely interpreted: "The gentleman would like an end piece *au jus* if you please." Pleased indeed!

Windsor

Homemade scones are another typical English culinary delight. These we enjoyed one afternoon outside

Windsor Castle. Matt had instructed us to board the train at Paddington Station and take the 30-minute ride to Windsor & Eton Central station in Berkshire. Once there, we made the steep climb on foot up to the castle. On the way we admired St. George's Chapel, the spiritual home of the Order of the Knights of the Garter. We were informed that the royal real estate is "designed in the Perpendicular Gothic style." *I say, Perpendicular Gothic. How brilliant!*

We wandered around the Upper and Lower Wards of the "largest inhabited castle in the world." The fact that the premises belonged to so many kings and queens from the year 900 turned the tour into a veritable history lesson.

Around lunchtime we decided to try some historical British scones. They were served with jam and "lashings of Devonshire clotted cream." Equally as reminiscent of past centuries was the steeped English tea. Jolly good!

Back in the capital, we spent an evening at the theatre in Piccadilly Circus in the West End. The show was "Cats" by Andrew Lloyd Webber, performed on a revolving stage at the New London Theatre. Tony, caught up in the excitement of the novel and imaginative theatrics, could hardly stop applauding. On my part, never having been able to relate to felines, the reaction was less enthusiastic. I had been more impressed by the nearby Church of St. Martin-in-the-Fields where Sir Neville Marriner recorded countless classical masterpieces. (Frankly, I am surprised to learn that the London production of "Cats" went on for 21 years, the second longest musical in West End history, surpassed only by *Les Misérables*.)

On Sunday morning we noticed in the tourist brochure that nothing seemed to be open. We approached the concierge and asked what do people do in London on a Sunday? The answer was instantaneous: "Sightsee!" It proved a good excuse to check off the sites that Matt had dictated. We attended Mass at Westminster Cathedral. "Dull" was the assessment. The Tower of London was "eerie," St. Paul's "grandiose," Parliament "stately," and the city itself "a fascinating and alluring metropolis."

Our round-trip airfare had been a bargain. We had booked a charter flight to and from Heathrow with a side trip to Spain in between. A local travel agent arranged return flight from Valencia to Gatwick; from there we were to take a bus to Heathrow. "Isn't that cutting it rather close?" we asked. "Not to worry," we were assured, "There's plenty of time to make your flight from Heathrow to the U.S."

We arrived at Heathrow's boarding gate only to be informed, "Your flight is presently taxiing for takeoff." *Bitte?* Tony exclaimed. "Tell them to stop! I have an important meeting tomorrow!" Tony tried to do a repeat of his Munich opera house routine to no avail. "Sir, you will have to purchase a ticket on tomorrow's flight."

There was no alternative but to dish out an amount larger than the original round-trip charter purchase price. Worse than that, we faced the expense of overnight hotel accommodations.

The weather didn't help matters either; it was raining cats (Spare me!) and dogs. I swear I spent every Pound

Sterling I had on the phone calling every hotel in the directory. "Sorry, we are fully booked," came the recurring response. "Let's just get a taxi," I suggested, "and ask the cabbie if he knows where we can find a room." Bingo! "Not a problem," replied the driver who soon enough dropped us off at a Victorian residence that rented flats to stranded foreigners. Of course, by the time we transferred our luggage we were thoroughly drenched, freezing and hoping that our next visit to the Continent would provide a more propitious ending.

Chapter Four: Paris Revisited

Our return to Paris several years after the whirlwind tour was much more enriching thanks to the guidance of an expert in all things French. Norma, a former parishioner and friend, had traveled the globe as an airline executive. Upon retirement she elected to settle down in her favorite city. Her hospitable nature and gracious personality prompted her to share with American friends the treasures of her adopted home.

Norma arranged for us to stay at a traditional Parisian hotel in the center of town. The first morning there was a knock at the door. Before we could get out of our beds a jovial maiden danced in balancing a breakfast tray with cups of hot *cafe au lait,* oven-fresh croissants, butter, jam and cream. *Merci, mademoiselle!* What a way to awaken! This is the real Paris!

Not quite. The real Paris was yet to unfold at the hands of Norma, our gracious hostess and guide. Her tours were exquisitely designed to highlight different districts of the sprawling metropolis. The first excursion started at the Eiffel Tower. From its height we took in at a glance all the venues we would explore the following days.

That evening we dined at a unique restaurant. We descended a winding staircase into a large cave-like environment with subdued lighting. The ambiance was exotic, the food elegant. When we surfaced, Norma led us on a night tour of L' Avenue des Champs-Elysees. No amount of champagne – or Asti Spumante – could have been more intoxicating.

Day two began with a visit to a neighborhood delicatessen. The plan was to purchase a picnic lunch that we would share in a park near the Louvre. The charming deli was a gourmand's paradise –baguettes, meats, cheeses, wines, fruit, exotic delicacies – and the pastries! Tony swooned with delight.

Our guide insisted on public transportation, especially the handsome and efficient underground Metro - and of course lots of legwork. We meandered through the monumental Basilique du Sacre-Coeur atop Montmartre, processed down the aisles of the stained-glass wonder of La Sainte Chapelle, stood in awe at Bonaparte's historic memorial. At Le Jardin du Luxembourg we paused to devour our delicious deli fare. Lastly, we ambled through the *Musée Louvre* with its 38,000 art objects from prehistory to the present. It is fittingly called the greatest museum in the world. Obviously it would take a lifetime to view its treasures. We enjoyed but a glance.

On another excursion, as we were approaching the modern mind-blowing Centre Pompidou museum, we had to ask Norma to stop so that we could catch our breath - it had been literally taken away by the sheer scale and impact of all the sites we visited. The experience had been utterly fascinating, exhilarating and culturally over the top! Personally, Norma's expeditions had the same effect as the carafes of Riesling on the Rhine!

Most spiritually enriching of all was the incomparable Cathedral of Notre Dame. Upon entering the Medieval temple, the religious heritage of the ages artfully embedded in the building's interior envelopes, embraces and enthralls the soul.

France is known as the eldest daughter of the Church for good reason. Over the centuries she was instrumental in spreading Christianity from the heart of Europe to outer reaches of the globe. It reminded Tony and me of our personal debt to the French priests who were the origin and source of our priestly formation - the Sulpician Fathers who had been our seminary professors and spiritual directors.

Our final Parisian pilgrimage, therefore, was to the Church of Saint-Sulpice in the Odeon Quarter of the 6th Arrondissement. It was there that in 1641 Jean-Jacques Olier founded the Society of Saint Sulpice dedicated to the education and formation of candidates for the Catholic priesthood. From this sacred spot a group of five theologians set out in 1898 for St. Patrick's Seminary in Menlo Park, California. Now, as two products of that institution, Tony and I were returning to pay homage and to give thanks for 12 years under Sulpician formation. We like to think that this French connection qualified us as honorary citizens of this remarkable metropolis.

Now it was time to bid *Adieu* to "Paree" – and to Norma a heartfelt *Merci beaucoup.* As we boarded the plane at Charles de Gaulle Airport we had no inkling that one day we would return to that terminal in the "fashion capital of the world" only to undergo a thorough "dressing down."

Chapter Five: Nightmare at De Gaulle

De Gaulle Airport was supposed to have been a brief and normal transfer point *en route* to Israel and other countries to the north. Tony was on a mini-sabbatical consisting of a month's study in the Holy Land concluding with another month's theological course at Louvain in Brussels. Sandwiched in between were scheduled visits to Greece, Hungary, Vienna, Kiev, Moscow and Leningrad. I was to be with him on the first two legs of the trip.

The day before we were to depart, President Ronald Reagan decided to bomb Libya (April 15, 1986). As a result, Colonel Muammar Gaddafi vowed to disrupt tourism in Europe and the Middle East. Any aircraft with passengers from hostile countries, he threatened, would be taken down! Tony refused to be intimidated by some "hysterical dictator halfway around the world." No, we would leave as planned.

When we arrived at San Francisco Airport for departure, security and military personnel were everywhere, as were bomb-sniffing guard dogs. We weaved our way through the "war zone" to the boarding platform. As we stepped into the United Airlines 747 we noticed a lot of empty seats in the cabin. Armed only with our determination and a travel bag stuffed with tickets, visas, hotel reservations and transport vouchers, we took off for Paris where we were to transfer to a flight on El Al, the Israeli airline.

Easier said than done. Finding the ticket counter for El Al at De Gaulle Airport proved a challenge. No one could or would tell us where it was located; they seemed to be keeping it a secret. Then it dawned on us: *Libya was an Arab country and an enemy of Israel. Gaddafi was a friend of the beleaguered Palestinians, including those in Israel – mainly in East Jerusalem. Anything Israeli-owned would be a prime target for Muammar's revengeful missiles!*

The ordeal was just beginning. After hauling luggage through interminable aisles and a maze of black curtains, we finally found El Al Airline's Check In. As at SFO, there were armed guards at every corner.

Tony and I were approached by Israeli agents and instructed to line up at two different stations. It soon became apparent that the two of us had been targeted as "suspicious." *What information had their computers spit up – two possible terrorists disguised as priests?* In Tony's case, it was easier to understand. His swarthy complexion and distinct facial features suggested a desert provenance. I recalled that on our first train ride over the German Alps a stranger sidled up to Tony, looked intently into his face and asked, "Irani?" "Nein," Tony replied, "Mexikaner!"

At my station, the agent asked for my packet of passages to the countries we had arranged to visit – including Communist Hungary and Russia. With a dramatic flourish he unfurled the stream of visas and vouchers and sarcastically asked, "Is this a typical itinerary for a priest?" Having been warned to expect provocative questions, I kept my cool. Feigning a chuckle, I asked back, "What do *you* consider a typical itinerary for a priest?" He did not respond; instead he indicated for me to follow him. *Oh, oh!*

The El Al agent ushered me into a room reserved for interrogations and body searches. Tony was already there. We were ordered to undress. Our clothing was meticulously inspected, as was our luggage - item by item. "What's this?" Tony was asked. "My camera." "Take a picture." "Of what?" "That wall." The suspicious device was declared legitimate. Tubes of toothpaste were squeezed empty. We sympathized with the innocent dispensers – our stomachs were suffering the same sensation!

After that humiliating episode we were placed in the custody of a female security guard. In the folds of her raincoat was a curious protrusion resembling the contours of an AK-47. She also carried the confiscated packets with our passports, documents and boarding passes. Briskly, she proceeded to marshal us to our plane. Visions of Wagner's ill-fated "Flying Dutchman" flashed before the mind.

It was then that my outrage, triggered by an overwhelming thirst, emboldened me. "Take me to Duty Free!" I demanded, "I need to buy some gin!" Our machine gun-toting nanny stopped and looked at me sternly. Realizing that I was really upset and determined, she relented and led us to the desired dispensary. Ushering us to the aisle lined with bottles of Gilbey's, Beefeater and Tanqueray, she watched as I deliberated upon a selection.

A sudden thought popped into my mind: *I think I'll get some brandy, too.* Impulsively I scurried off to find the whiskey section. Momentarily distracted, our armed escort hadn't seen me slip away. When she realized I wasn't there she freaked out, calling for reinforcements. When I was found grabbing two pints of Hennessy I was abruptly hustled over to the cashier.

Tony and I were then muscled onto our idling transport. Our military shepherdess handed us our documents and escorted us into the cabin packed with mostly Israeli passengers. There were two unoccupied seats: one in the front for me, and the other for Tony in the rear – between two bearded Hassidic rabbis.

Chapter Six: Students in Israel

East Jerusalem

We settled into our accommodations at the Anglican academy situated in the Palestinian section of the Holy City. That night Tony confessed that he might have been responsible for the hostile detention and interrogation in Paris. "When the agent at the ticket counter asked me our destination I answered 'EAST Jerusalem.'" Remorsefully he muttered, "I guess I just should have answered 'St. George's College.'"

Some time back, Tony had come across a brochure announcing a three-week course entitled "Worship Places in the Bible." It included the following description:

> Situated only a few minutes from the Old City of Jerusalem, St. George's provides year-round courses that combine academic study, spirituality and travel. There is no substitute for a St. George's course. In Jerusalem you will visit the different quarters of the Old City including the Church of the Resurrection, the Dome of the Rock and the Temple Mount. In Bethlehem you will visit the Church of the Nativity and the Shepherd's Fields. In Galilee you will focus on the ministry of Jesus in Nazareth and around the Sea of Galilee.

The college was established during the British Mandate before the formation of the State of Israel. One of its purposes was to educate Palestinians living in East

Jerusalem. Today the College continues to provide academic courses to outsiders interested in the history, archeology and theology of the Holy Land.

Our Jerusalem classmates were 30 eager students from all over the world including scholars from England, ministers from Nova Scotia, seminarians from Jordan. Much of the time we were taken on fieldtrips to distant locales associated with biblical shrines and places of worship as mentioned in the brochure. On our return trip from Galilee, for example, we were among the few buses allowed to travel to the Jordan River via the Golan Heights, a militarized zone. On these excursions, as in the classroom, instructors provided useful background information from biblical, historical and archeological sources.

The highlight of our stay in Jerusalem, however, was the celebration of the rituals of Orthodox Holy Week.

Palm Sunday Eve

Tony likes to retell the story of our fieldtrip to Lazarus' tomb in Bethany. It was on the Saturday before Palm Sunday. The Bible records that Martha and Mary's dead brother Lazarus had been in his tomb for four days when Jesus arrived. As was the custom at the time, corpses were interred in a cave-like mausoleum which was then sealed with a large stone. "Take away the stone," Jesus ordered. "Then he cried out in a loud voice 'Lazarus, come out!' The dead man came out, tied hand and foot with burial bands." (John 11:43-44)

Today, pilgrims are allowed to enter the cave and descend into the crypt where Lazarus is believed to have been buried. Most visitors stay only a few minutes. I was smitten with the mystique of the locale and decided to purchase a memento from a makeshift shop in the corner. My recollection is that that I got into a long conversion with the vendor who obviously wanted to make a sale. I hadn't heard the order to vacate the premises. By the time I was ready to exit, the door to the entrance was tightly shut. Outside I heard people singing. Then I heard the sound of someone unlatching the door. I opened it and stepped out.

Tony's version is that he and everyone was told to surface because the annual sacred liturgy was about to begin. Every year on that date, the Orthodox patriarch along with an entourage of priests and deacons congregate in front of the tomb of Lazarus to commemorate and reenact the miracle.

Tony and all our classmates were in the crowd as the eminent prelate sang the ancient prayers and listened to the deacon's solemn chanting of St. John's account of the event. It was precisely when the deacon ceremoniously removed the latch to the opening and pronounced Christ's command, "Lazarus, come out," that the door suddenly opened and out came I! Tony says that at my unexpected appearance, the class "wit" - a scholarly English liturgist - leaned over to him and in his cultured Oxford accent whispered, "Your friend is now a relic!"

During the week, the class was taken to another subterranean gravesite. This unique venue was not opened to the public. However, St. George's College had access to it because of its close ties with the Armenian Patriarchate of Jerusalem. The cave was located in the Church of the Holy Sepulchre, directly under the site of Christ's Crucifixion. As students of the College we were allowed to descend into the Chapel of St. Helena (Constantine's mother) which is in the exclusive custody of the Armenians. From this chapel, an additional stairway led down to a rock-hewn cave known as the Chapel of the Invention of the Cross. Centuries-old relics of early Christian devotion framed the walls like scenes from the Stations of the Cross. The privileged visit provided a perfect prelude to the approaching *Triduum*, Holy Week's most sacred celebrations.

Holy Thursday

On Holy Thursday Tony and I set out in the early morning to look for the room of the Last Supper called the *Cenaculum*. When we arrived near the site a Franciscan friar informed us that the shrine was closed. Jewish archeologists, he explained, had recently discovered under the original Christian shrine the more ancient burial site of King David. Consequently, the structure had been taken over by the government for restoration.

However, poking around, we discovered that no one was working that day; the upper room was vacant and unguarded. So, we climbed the stairs and found ourselves in an environment not unlike that depicted in Da Vinci's famous fresco of the Last Supper. Everything was in the process of being remodeled. The vaulted ceiling was freshly painted and the floor entirely empty of furniture.

Awed and inspired, we began singing Eucharistic hymns in Latin: *Panis Angelicus*, O *Salutaris Hostia, Tantum Ergo Sacramentum*. The acoustics were remarkable; they created a reverberating chamber that transported us back to that first Holy Thursday when Jesus sang psalms joined by the voices of his disciples. It was a miracle we weren't discovered by Jewish archeologists searching for the royal remains of David the original composer and singer of psalms!

Good Friday

The next day happened to be my 50th birthday – a milestone I was dreading. In fact, I was probably undergoing a mild midlife crisis. That my birthday fell on Good Friday seemed appropriate enough! I spent the day at Gethsemane, the garden shrine where Jesus prayed and sweated blood as he endured his own ordeal.

Several priests were hearing confessions. I entered the confessional and told the confessor how confused I was. I'll never forget his response: "Thank you for coming. Do you see that stone over there? That's where Jesus suffered his agony." He paused, then commented, "St. Luke tells us that 'to strengthen him an angel from heaven appeared to him.'" (Luke 22:43). The priest blessed me and dismissed me with these words: "My prayer for you, my son, is that an angel will appear to strengthen you."

When I returned to my room at St. George's a bouquet of 50 red roses was sitting on my nightstand. The card read: "Happy BD. After fifty, life gets rosier!" It was from an "angel" back home.

Tony spent the day among the throngs on the *Via Dolorosa* observing the traditional Stations of the Cross. I suspected at the time that he was also checking out the merchandise in the countless stores and stalls that line the hallowed route. Since neither of us like to carry a camera, Tony was fond of picking up postcards and mementos everywhere we went. His favorite items were T-shirts and sports apparel with printed logos and emblems heralding the place of origin. Thus, when not in clerical garb, he became a sort of walking billboard/travelogue. On the other hand, my suspicion may have been merely a symptom of my confused state of mind.

Holy Saturday/Easter

The climactic experience of Orthodox Holy Week was Holy Saturday and Easter morning. We were awakened at three in the morning and transported to the Church of the Holy Sepulchre. We would be among the privileged to witness the "miracle of the Holy Fire."

At the appointed time the Greek Orthodox Patriarch processed into the sacred chamber. There he was searched by Israeli authorities for any utensils that might ignite a fire. He then entered the holiest site in all Christendom, The Tomb (sepulcher) of Christ called the Aedicule. After a short time, His Most Godly Beatitude reappeared with several candles miraculously aflame with the Holy Fire. The moment commemorated Christ's resurrection from the dead. The congregation exploded into cheers of joy and wild applause. Tapers lit from the Holy Fire turned the sacred precinct into a lantern illuminating the recesses of nearby Calvary and the tomb "where they laid him" and which was now declared "empty." A blaze of light documented the moment! *Christos anesti!* Christ is risen! Alleluia, Alleluia!

+++

The Gospels relate that soon after his resurrection Jesus appeared to his disciples on several occasions. The first was on the road to a "village seven miles from Jerusalem called Emmaus." (Luke 24:13). It was there that he revealed himself as alive and still a presence in their lives.

Appropriately, the final fieldtrip of the course at St. George's College was an exploration of that site. To every student's surprise, our British lecturer announced that we would be journeying not to one single location but to four. Each was seven miles distant and each claimed to be the original Emmaus.

The first was a Franciscan monastery that featured year-round retreats and spiritual counseling. The second was a former convent converted into a center for creative arts, housing painters, sculptors, musicians and dancers, providing them with resources to produce works of beauty. The third site featured a community of mixed families, Christians, Jews and Muslims, successfully living together in peace and harmony, with integrated government and social activities. The fourth Emmaus startled us. It was a bleak uninhabited landscape, a heap of rubble and total devastation where the homes of native Palestinians had been bulldozed and leveled.

On the ride back to the college, our insightful instructor suggested that perhaps each location had earned the right to call itself Emmaus. "Christ," she declared thoughtfully, "continues to show that he is alive and present in institutions promoting spiritual growth, in artistic works of beauty, in efforts at cultural and religious co-existence, and even – as the wounds on Christ's risen body attest – in experiences of conflict, desolation and blight."

+++

As Tony and I prepared to leave St. George's, the office secretary singled me out and announced, "There's a phone call for you from the States." It was Colleen Parrish from Oakland. She and Bill would not be joining us in Greece as planned. "We've canceled our flight." (As had two million other would-be travelers.) "Too risky," she explained, "with that mad Libyan leader on the loose! Oh, and by the way," she concluded, "we hope you canceled your trip to Russia ... all those rumors about a catastrophic explosion! Hurry home!"

"Holy Land"
Worshipping at sacred shrines in Galilee and Jerusalem as students in Israel

Chapter Seven: Greco-Austro-Hungarian Interlude

Greece

After we finished our studies in Israel we resumed our original itinerary. All airports were still on high alert. The Gaddafi scare lingered and now a new nervousness pervaded transport hubs. The exception was Greece. When we arrived at Athens International, armed soldiers were everywhere. The strange thing was, they were either playing cards or on coffee break - to a man, all were smoking cigarettes. Judging from the haze floating throughout the terminal, puffing tobacco must be a national pastime. Despite official security regulations, the Greek guards, seated at their gaming tables, looked up from time to time and waved passengers along - lit cigarettes in hand.

As we stepped out of the smoky terminal and into the open-air - gasping for oxygen, we walked into a metropolis blanketed in smog. This environmental hazard, we were informed, had afflicted the city for years, corroding the Acropolis and munching away at the ancient monuments. There were rumors that the city fathers were as motivated and concerned as the airport security personnel; they too, it was claimed, spent their days playing cards and smoking cigarettes. As a result, the pollution continued to eat away at the country's Hellenic heritage.

Hoping to escape suffocation, Tony and I boarded a train to Corinth, a breezy coastal port city 48 miles west of the Capital. Mistake! It would have been smarter to book a ride to Hades. First of all, the locomotive was a coal-devouring monster that spewed billows of black soot in all directions. Secondly, the beast stalled midway, stranding us for two hours. We sat there helplessly trapped with no way to exit. Thirdly, everybody in our car took to playing cards and smoking cigarettes! Ugh! As Tony always says when overwhelmed - "I died!" *Died and gone to Hades*, was my assessment!

The air - and our lungs - cleared up when we boarded a ship bound for Mykonos in the Aegean that locals named The Island of the Winds. Upon disembarking we took a casual stroll through the town's small commercial quarter. It was deserted. We soon found out why. A merchant standing idly in the doorway of his shop espied the two of us as we approached his store. Overjoyed at the sight of potential clients, he started jumping up and down. "You come in here!" he commanded, "You buy something!" Sensing our hesitation, he explained, "No one come for months. Need to feed kids!"

Obviously, the Libyan threat and whatever else was curtailing global tourism was taking its toll on remote and vulnerable entrepreneurs. Generous to a fault and the original "soft touch," Tony stacked up on T-shirts, sizes S – L for the nephews, XXL for himself, and necklaces of various lengths for the nieces.

We continued bolstering the island's economy by patronizing its enticing restaurants. Nothing tastes as good as a Greek salad created in Greece. The distinctive flavor of home-grown greens, tomatoes, olives, cucumbers, onions, bell peppers, oregano and Feta cheese can't be replicated anywhere else in the world. The same holds true for Greek dishes like Moussaka, Gyros, Kadaifi, Dolma, Baklava - not to mention Retsina Wine and dance-inducing Ouzo. Unlike the "train ride to Hades," the climate and cuisine on the island of Mykonos transported us to a make-believe Mount Olympus.

Hungary

From the Greek isles we continued our nautical odyssey by cruising on the River Danube to Communist-ruled Budapest. Since we were on our way to the Soviet Union, we figured that a stop at a socialist republic could prepare us for our imminent visit to Russia.

Sure enough: The main marketplace and transport hub in Budapest was called Moscow Square. It was teeming with illegal workers, gypsy street vendors and flower sellers as well as a host of pubs and cafes. To our great fortune, Judy Lavar was there to meet us. Judy was our bishop's chef and cathedral cook who was born in Hungary and lived in Budapest until forced to flee the Soviet Suppression of 1956. She enthusiastically showed us the Capital's impressive landmarks. Among the grandest was the restored and recently opened Hungarian State Opera House glowing in Renaissance glitz and glamour. Judy and her actress friend Zoe acted as our "dates" when we attended a memorable performance of Mozart's *Così Fan Tutte.*

The opulence of the opera house, however, stood in stark contrast to the real condition of the impoverished and crippled economy – and of a struggling populace. Its national currency, the Forint, was worthless outside the Soviet sphere. Citizens craved U. S. dollars - provided mostly by tourists. As a result, Tony and I became targets of the so-called independent foreign exchange operators. "You have dollars to exchange? I give you higher rate than the banks." They count out a handful of Forints, snatch your outstretched $100 greenback or signed Traveler's Check and sprint away. The victim is left with the equivalent of $10! Lesson learned.

The Hungarian Soviet Republic had one positive resource and lucrative asset: It was Eastern Europe's "bargain basement" for westerners. Tony couldn't believe the dirt-cheap prices for quality merchandise – all Made in the U.S.S.R. He loaded up on beaver fur Russian Trooper Style hats, and exceptional amber gemstone jewelry. I purchased two high grade black leather jackets. As a result, our suitcases were bulging with treasures from the East as we set off for the next leg of our mini sabbatical.

Austria

In Vienna we attempted to confirm our reservations to Kiev, Moscow and Leningrad. When the Austrian travel agent learned of our intended destination she was horrified. "Do me a favor," she pleaded, "Forget about traveling to Russia." She informed us of the explosion of the nuclear facility at Chernobyl near Kiev and its continuing meltdown. "Here in Austria," she said, "we have been instructed to keep our children off any green grass, and not to let them eat ice cream. The radioactive fallout is all over Europe!"

Evidently it was even contaminating the cows! At any rate, she counseled, "You should check with *Intourist,* the official Russian travel bureau."

To our request to speak to an agent, the young receptionist at *Intourist* responded in English, "No one speak English." I then said in French, *Nous voulons parler avec un agent de voyage.* "No one speak *Français."* *Queremos hablar con un agente...* "No speak *Español."*

Tony then reiterated our demand in a lengthier litany of languages. To each recitation the Russian secretary answered "No speak." Finally, folding his arms and looking the girl straight in the eye, he clearly enunciated in English: "We will not leave here until we speak to someone about our reservations to KIEV!"

Bingo! Before we could say *bitte,* we are being escorted into a large conference room with a long table surrounded by a dozen chairs. In walked a tall, hefty official who seated himself at the head of the table; Tony and I had been given seats at the opposite end. There seemed to be a mile separating us.

Before either of us could utter a word, we heard a low, strong bass voice utter: "Nah-sing happen in Kiev." "We understand that," we responded. "However, we wish to change our reservations and perhaps go directly to Moscow." "Nah-sing happen in Kiev!" echoed the voice in a higher register. "Of course! All we want to do is investigate the possibility of visiting some other city in your magnificent country." "Nah-sing happen in Kiev!"

roared the voice – somewhere in the contralto range. Not willing to endure a soprano rendition of "Nah-sing happen in Kiev!" we decided to thank our host and get back to our hotel for a needed nap!

Tony immediately fell asleep; I could not. Fully awake and disappointed with our failure at *Intourist*, I phoned the Russian travel agency in San Francisco where I had obtained special visas and purchased airfare. To my surprise an agent informed me that she had just received a Telex stating that tourists destined for Kiev would be rerouted. However, the individuals would have no choice but to go wherever the Russian government determined. It sounded as if one might end up in the Crimea on a whim of a Communist official in Moscow. When Tony awoke, I informed him of the news from San Francisco. "Do you want to go the Crimea – or maybe Siberia?" I asked. "No way! Let's go to Spain instead!" *¡Vale, vale!*

Chapter Eight: A Family Album of Spain

It would not be our first trip to the Iberian Peninsula. We had been there twice before. The first time was in that whirlwind tour of Europe in 1969 when the country was in the grip of the powerful military dictatorship of Generalissimo Francisco Franco. He had attempted to unite 17 provinces by, among other things, imposing *Castellano,* the Castilian dialect, as the common language for all Spaniards. The move might have been good for tourism and commerce but it became an odious burden for the diverse population with multiple dialects.

Franco ruled through censorship, coercion, imprisonment of enemies, and other totalitarian measures that suppressed creativity and strangled initiative. With police stationed at every corner, one could walk the streets at any time of day or night. Everyone, however, resident and tourist alike, felt constricted and sealed in.

Thankfully for Tony and me, our stay had been brief but long enough to make us realize that despite the troubles back home, we were at least free to deal with them openly without fear of excessive repression. This lesson alone was worth the visit.

Alcalá de Chivért, Province of Castellón, Valencian Community

When we returned after Franco's death (1975), Spain was transitioning to a more democratic constitutional monarchy. One could sense that the oppressive lid had been lifted. The genie that had given birth to Flamenco, bullfighting and Salvador Dalí was out of the bottle!

Our exposure to the changing climate resulted from our stay with a family in the vicinity of Valencia. Sócrates Mañez, his wife Milagros and their two sons Manuel and Francisco Javier lived in Alcalá de Chivért on the Mediterranean coast. Sócrates' brother was a Franciscan priest working with us in Oakland. In opening their hearts and home to us they provided an enriching, first-hand experience of authentic Spanish life, culture and home cooking.

Sócrates was genuine, pure-bred Iberian "bull," Milagros the epitome of a dedicated, resourceful wife, mother and homemaker; the boys typical red-blooded modern youths. Curiously, among themselves they communicated in *Valenciano,* their native dialect; with us they spoke in Castilian. The boys were sternly instructed: ¡*Cuando los padres están, solo se habla Castellano, ¡Vale, vale!*

Along with the home in the city, the Mañez family owned *Apartamentos San Miguel* where they resided during the summer months. Located in the backyard of the units stretched the warm waters of the Mediterranean Sea. It was there that on a Sunday morning we awoke to find Doña Milagros in the sand stoking a fire inside some stacked bricks. On top of this makeshift oven she had placed a large *paellera,* a curved pan three feet in circumference. The fire would be kept burning for several hours as she created her version of *Paella mixta a la Valenciana.*

Fascinated, we watched as she heated olive oil in which she seared an assortment of meats: chicken, rabbit and various sausages, including links of *morcilla* made from pig's blood. She sautéed the mix until golden brown – except the bloody *morcillas* that turned black. Setting the cooked meats aside, she proceeded to stir in an array of onions, garlic and bell peppers until tender, adding grated tomatoes and dry seasoning.

We didn't get a chance to witness our hostess complete her masterpiece that awaited the signature ingredients of rice seasoned with saffron – and who knows what other exotic secrets? Sócrates appeared and announced that he and the boys were going to take us on a tour of nearby points of interest.

The first was a visit to the castle of Peníscola, the residence of the anti-pope Benedict XIII better known as Papa Luna. (In 1400 there were three different claimants to the Chair of Peter. This one was eventually declared a schismatic and excommunicated by the Council of Constance in 1417.) Being of Spanish origin Papa Luna fled to his native land and ended his years in the castle we were visiting.

The last site Sócrates selected was more for the benefit of his two sons. Evidently, they had been pestering him for the chance to drive the family vehicle. "You see that road there?" he snorted. "Two days ago, a speeding drunk crashed his car and was killed." Then he thundered, *Quedó carbonizado!* "He ended up a piece of carbon!" Tony and I exchanged a giggle-suppressed glance, marveling at the descriptive paternal warning.

We arrived back at the apartment around noon. The *paellera* in the backyard was brimming with a mound of saffron-laced rice with steaming vegetables, meats and seafood. Milagros was adding final garnishes to the delectable heap that could feed the crew of a Spanish galleon.

While we waited for guests to arrive including *el Señor Cura* (parish priest), Sócrates showed Tony and his younger son Francisco Javier how to make aioli, a type of mayonnaise. While Tony slowly poured a steady stream of olive oil into a bowl, the boy furiously whisked the mixture to the desired consistency while Papa added minced garlic and seasonings. To see the three generations studiously concocting the age-old recipe spoke volumes of how traditions are preserved.

Around 2 in the afternoon, 12 of us sat down at table to share - and share everyone did. The rich paella and flowing Rioja unleashed each diner's tongue and viewpoint. There were 11 males and one female – Doña Milagros. Even though outnumbered, she nevertheless held her own, expressing vociferous opinions regarding the role of women in the new Spanish society. For her feminist views Sócrates declared her *¡mentalizada!*

The local parish priest along with his two drivers heatedly voiced views on socialism, religion and democracy – as did everybody else. Tony eagerly got into the fray, assuming a distinctly Spanish accent, punctuating his comments with *¡Vale, vale! Pués, hombre!*

All the while, bottles of Rioja kept surfacing from some bottomless cellar. By dinner's end I counted 12 of them – all empty. As the sun began to drown in the Mediterranean, Sócrates announced that the hour had arrived for *La Queimada*, "The Burning." *Oh dear, are we all going to end up like that drunk motorist?*

A large bowl containing a half kilo of sugar was placed in the center of the table. A metal pitcher of hot, black viscous coffee was poured over the sugar. Finally, two bottles of rum were emptied into the mixture. Striking a long match, the host ceremoniously set the concoction ablaze. When the flaming alcohol had finished cooking the sugar-sweetened coffee, there remained a black syrupy substance which we all cheerfully consumed. We were told later that *La Queimada* is a traditional ritual designed to ward off hangovers. It actually worked! Despite the case of Rioja consumed, every diner rose from the table completely sober.

We had sat down at 2 in the afternoon; it was 10 at night when we reluctantly left the table. The drivers escorted *el Señor Cura* to his car. Little Francisco Javier was scraping the bottom of the *paellera* for crusty remnants of the burnt rice (*socarrat* or *arroz carbonizado*). Every Spanish youngster knows that's the best part of paella. The best part for Tony had been the bloody *morcillas*, which he devoured with ghoulish gusto.

After dinner Tony and I went for a stroll along the seashore, refreshing our feet in the waters of the glistening

Mediterranean. As we raised our eyes, we shivered to see glowing in the star-filled firmament, a white-hot harvest moon! *Flashback to Coblenz and Máni's full moon. Bitte! ¡Vale, Vale!*

+++

The following evening, we had a shock. There, standing at the door was our colleague Bill Cieslak! Bill was a Franciscan Capuchin monk with the personality of a fun-loving Friar Tuck. He was also a faculty member of the Franciscan School of Theology in Berkeley. It was there that we had casually mentioned that we would be in Spain at the same time he planned to be at a European conference. "Maybe we can meet up," he mused. "Leave me a copy of your itinerary."

By golly, here he was – at 11:30 at night! He explained that he had traveled by train from Austria; it had taken 34 hours. When he got to Alcalá he went to the hotel and asked, "Where are the two padres from California?" No one knew. So, he rented a room and went to bed. At 11 he was awakened by a knock at the door. It was a nephew of Sócrates. He offered to drive him to his uncle's apartments where the two padres from California were staying. Now having found us, the Polish-American monk was eager to accompany his Spanish-speaking comrades on a "conquest of Spain."

Chapter Nine: More Snapshots of Spain

So instead of Kiev we found ourselves once again in Alcalá de Chivért at the home of Sócrates and Milagros Mañez. The intervening years had conferred on all of us a few graying hairs. The two boys were now grown men. The couple greeted us with cheerful news: "How fantastic you've come at this time; Manuel is getting married next week! What a gift to have the two of you to perform the marriage of our eldest son to his beloved fiancée Nieves!"

We were delighted at the announcement and readily accepted the invitation to preside at the religious ceremony. However, we knew that the family would be busy with wedding preparations. Not wanting to burden them with having to entertain unexpected guests, we decided to take a little side trip. We would return, we assured everyone, in time for the nuptials. Our destination: to visit friends in Catalonia.

Figueres, Province of Girona, Catalonian Community

Here's the story of how I made friends with a couple from Girona, a region close to the French border at the foot of the Pyrenees. It starts in Oakland, California. I'm working at my desk at the cathedral rectory. My phone rings. "Father, there is a gentleman on the line who says he wants to get married – today! Shall I put him through?" OK.

"Father, this may sound strange, but let me explain. My name is Carlos Cosbó. I am in San Francisco with my fiancée

Dolores. You might call us adventurers. We are addicted to traveling the world six months of the year. This year we decided to get married in San Francisco. We both left from Spain but in opposite directions; Dolores went East and I came West. We agreed to meet on this date and exchange marriage vows. We have the canonical paperwork and documents provided by our priest in Girona. The problem is: We can't find any priest in the archdiocese who is available. We were wondering if you could help?"

I answered: "That is the most creative wedding plans I have ever heard! Two lovers circling the globe to join hands and hearts in San Francisco! I'll tell you what: Come to the Oakland cathedral this morning. I will examine the paperwork and if all is in order, I will marry you at our noon Mass."

They came, I saw, they conquered.

Needing two official witnesses, I phoned Fidel and Rosa Maria and instructed them to dress up for a wedding: "You are going to be best man and maid of honor for Carlos and Dolores Cosbó from Madre España."

Our Catalonian couple returned to their country to undertake enterprises that would fund future semi-annual globe-trotting adventures. It wasn't long before I received a letter and a brochure that read:

> *"Café del Port - Right on main harbor Ampuria Brava. Your new cool spot and snack bar in the port just off the slipway. Come and meet Carlos*

and Dolores your friendly English-speaking Catalonians who besides serving on you can offer hints on anything concerning the area."

The letter was a personal invitation not only to explore the region but to visit and stay at their parents' ranch in Jerez de la Frontera in the province of Girona. As a meeting spot they suggested a nearby village called Figueres. So that is where Tony and I headed as we boarded a train in Alcalá de Chivért and sped past Barcelona to the hometown of Salvador Dalí.

The *Theatre-Museo Dalí* in Figueres is not only a museum, but as its title states, a theater; a venue where the dramatic, the highly imaginative, the grandiose is on display and in "architectural performance." And a theater under whose stage is buried the "cultural icon of the bizarre and the surreal."

To experience Figueres and the works of its native son is to tap into that part of the Iberian soul that has inspired intrepid individuals to break through the ordinary and launch out into the outer limits of human discovery – no matter how unimaginable. One thinks of the likes of fellow artist Antoni Gaudí of Barcelona, and of Ferdinand and Isabella of Castilla, the impetus behind the expeditions of "crazy" Christopher Columbus.

As we were winding up our mind-blowing tour through Dali's Theatre-Museum, Carlos and Dolores arrived. After warm greetings and catch-up talk, we drove to the family farm in Jerez de la Frontera. They introduced me to their parents as "the priest who married us in California," and Tony as "the padre who came to marry the couple in Alcalá." After a tour of the dairy and cheese production facilities and animal-raising enclosures, we were treated to the freshest and home-grown feast that one can imagine – with of course lots of ¡*Vale, vale!* conversation and carafes of red Rioja.

On the way back to the train station, Carlos and Dolores pointed out their cool spot and snack bar conveniently located in the heart of endless rows of apartment houses rented by vacationing Germans every summer. "When the northern migration is over," they announced, "We will resume our globe-trotting." As we waved our goodbyes Carlos shouted, "Maybe we will see you in Oakland in time to celebrate our anniversary!"

Back in Alcalá, the wedding festivities of Manuel and Nieves began with a religious ceremony. Tony and I bestowed the Church's solemn Nuptial Blessing as bride and groom promised to be true to each other in good times and in bad, in sickness and in health, and to love and honor one another all the days of their lives. The rituals were followed by a spectacular reception in an upscale restaurant overlooking the Mediterranean. The Sea seemed to sparkle and dance in response to the ¡*Vale, vale!* champagne toasts offered by family and friends. Finally, Tony and I joined Sócrates, Milagros and Nieves' parents in offering a departing blessing as the couple left for their honeymoon and a new life as Señor y Señora Manuel Mañez.

It was also time for Tony and me to undertake our separate journeys: I back to the States, and he to the next round of studies in Belgium. As we headed for the airport we reflected on our experiences in Israel, Greece, Hungary and Vienna. We both agreed on one thing: We had made the right decision to come back to Spain – even if Nah-sing happen in Kiev!

Valencia

There is one final snapshot to include in this album of Spain: that of another genius- generating city with its native son. The city is Valencia, the genius artist, sculptor, engineer and world-renowned architect, Santiago Calatrava.

Valencia is an ancient port city on the western Mediterranean. The showpiece of this third-largest metropolitan area of Spain is Santiago Calatrava's futuristic City of Arts and Sciences, a sprawling complex of stunning buildings and spaces including a planetarium, opera house, parkway of native flora, oceanographic center and museum. Like every visitor, Tony and I we were blown away by the architectural wonder that has been declared "one of the 12 treasures of Spain." What made the experience even more compelling was the fact that we had become personally acquainted with its principal creator.

Here's how that happened. After an earthquake had destroyed its cathedral, the Diocese of Oakland invited several noted architects to submit original renderings to replace the demolished structure. I was a member of the committee that chose Calatrava's design for the projected new Cathedral of Christ the Light. Because I was the more fluent Spanish-speaker in the group, I became a liaison between the diocese and the architect. As a result, Santiago and I developed a personal friendship that eventually included his charming wife and four gifted children.

When Santiago and Robertina celebrated their 25th wedding anniversary, they asked me to offer a private Mass. It took place at my parish in El Cerrito, California. The couple renewed their marriage vows witnessed by their three sons Michael, Gabriel and Rafael, and their six-year-old daughter Sophia, who received her First Holy Communion.

Sadly, the diocese ultimately rejected Calatrava's masterful design due to internal disputes. It was a tremendous disappointment. Yet despite the regrettable outcome, our friendship continued, sustained by genuine affection and enriched by Tony's cheerful diplomacy.

As an aside, I should state that Tony's sunny disposition and love for life served to defuse tension in situations of stress and potential conflict. These same qualities made him an ideal traveling companion. Tony loves to laugh and his laughter engenders a sense of joviality that in turn creates a sense of ease. In theology we would say he possessed the charism of joy. In fact, his motto is *Paz y Alegría*, qualities he radiates – except when he gets carried away by beauty or bombast; then, he embodies them.

+++

Our album of Spain includes snapshots of families from different regions: the Mañez and Calatrava from the coastal province of Valencia, and the Cosbó from Catalonia. Now it's time to add mementos from the interior province of Andalucía, birthplace of Flamenco and bullfighting.

"Spain"
The Mañez Wedding Reception (seated) Nieves, Manuel,
Milagros, Sócrates, Tony (standing), Osuna

Chapter Ten: Surveying Seville and Surroundings

To situate our first visit to Seville we have to backtrack a bit. Bill Cieslak had appeared unexpectedly at the Mañez apartments; he volunteered to join Tony and me in our "conquest" of Spain.

After grateful goodbyes to our friends in Alcalá, the three of us headed for the capital of Andalusia. Friar Bill informed us that there were Franciscan monasteries throughout Spain. We should start by staying at the famous convent in the center of Seville. The three branches of the Franciscan Order have a rule, he pointed out: One is never to refuse hospitality to a fellow monk – and his companions.

Bill rang the bell at the front entrance of the ancient *Convento Franciscano.* A friar in his late thirties welcomed us with a smile and a mischievous twinkle in his eye – a trait not lost on Bill. He identified himself as Fray Antonio. Bill then introduced himself as a Capuchin from California and asked for lodging. We soon discovered that Fray Antonio was the only young monk among the handful of others who proved to be relics of a bygone era. "Very few vocations in Spain," explained the aged Prior who had hobbled over to verify Bill's credentials. Ambling slowly down the deserted corridors he ushered us to our cells. The cloisters and enormous halls seemed to have been abandoned. Tony's sensitive nose detected an odor emanating from the courtyard. *Huele a viejo,* he muttered, "Smells like rot."

Forget the smell. Bill was determined to discover and experience the "soul of Seville." He conceived a cunning plot: "I am going to invite the Prior to go with us into town tonight," he announced. When approached, the seasoned superior answered: "We are not allowed to go out at night. Besides," he added, "the *portero* locks all entrances to the monastery at 9 o'clock."

It was then that Bill recalled the twinkle in Fray Antonio's eye. Cornering him in the refectory, Bill whispered, "Would you like to join us tonight? We want to explore the sights of Seville." ¡*Vale, vale!* replied the smiling friar. Then Bill inquired, "How will we get back in? I'm told that the doors are locked at 9." "Not a problem," asserted the co-conspirator, "I'm the *portero*." With a twinkle he produced the proof: "keeper of the keys." Bill asked if we should hire a taxi. "No need," answered our accomplice, "I will call a friend who has a car. We will leave at 9 – right after I lock the doors."

A Volkswagen Beetle was waiting for us in the dark. Somehow, we all squeezed in and headed for our night tour of Seville. It turned into a "nightclub" tour of Seville. Our driver Aurelio, whom Brother Antonio had called at the last minute, kept reminding his friend that he had to get back to his wife who expected him for supper. As it turned out, he never did make it home. His Franciscan buddy kept convincing him to take us to another nightclub.

The mischievous twinkle in the porter's eye belied a deep acquaintance with Seville's nightlife and its signature cultural contribution – *el Flamenco*. Two particular venues in the cradle of the native dance proved especially entertaining. The first was an intimate performance hall where authentic gypsies displayed their mastery of down-home Flamenco. The costumes were simple, the guitar and singing haunting and the dancing electric. The overall experience was earthy, raw and edgy – like the choreography of a bullfight.

After that exhilarating experience, Fray Antonio ordered his friend, still insisting on getting home to his wife, to drive us to a more colorful venue - one with a show and a bar. "Someplace more typical of the city's high-spirited, outgoing and inclusive nature." The spacious club specialized in elaborate *espectáculos* on a large stage with professional lighting. The main act was a chorus line of gorgeous dancers in flamboyant, tight-fitting gowns with long ruffled trains.

The establishment also encouraged audience participation. The room was packed with people of all ages, from toddlers to grannies. In between performances by the gorgeous dancers, everyone including toddlers and grannies exploded onto the stage or into the aisles to perform their own *Sevillians* with loud handclapping and shouts of ¡Olé, olé!

During these breaks the gorgeous chorus line would congregate at the bar. That's where some of them surrounded Tony and inquired about his provenance and "availability." Luckily Fray Antonio's twinkling eye noticed the exchange and rescued his namesake. Taking him aside, he enlightened Tony as to the provenance of the gorgeous dancers – Villa Transvestite! *¡Vale, vale!*

+++

Palos de la Frontera

Before departing Seville, we visited the historic Franciscan monastery called *La Rábida*. It is located in Palos de la Frontera, an hour's drive from the capital. This is where Christopher Columbus consulted with the Franciscan friars regarding plans for organizing an expedition of discovery. And it was from Palos de la Frontera that three ships, the *Niña*, *Pinta* and *Santa Maria*, set sail on August 3, 1492, for parts unknown.

As we were driving back to Seville, Tony reminded us of an incident that took place at the first Flamenco performance venue. After the show we ran into the principal guitarist. We told him how much we had enjoyed the performance. He asked us, *¿Y vosotros, de donde sois?* "And you, where are you from?" "From California," we replied. *¡Ah, aquellas lindas tierras del mundo nuevo!* "Ah," he chanted, "Those lovely lands of the New Word!"

NEW world? What happened to the last 500 years? Well, I guess you just can't dampen the pride of these sons of Conquistadores! And we who live in the New World should continue exploring it ourselves. Good idea. ¡Vale, vale!

PART II

Adventures in the "New World"

Chapter Eleven: California Nuggets

California is a state of stunning scenic beauty and rich cultural heritage. Tony and I have had memorable experiences exploring its treasures: the rugged Mendocino coastline; Lake Shasta and Dam with its fishing and water sports; the award-winning vineyards of Sonoma and Napa Valleys; the winter ski resorts of the Sierra Nevada; the San Joaquin Valley, "the richest agricultural region the world has ever known;" the incomparable waterfalls and monumental promontories of Yosemite National Park; the Los Angeles metropolis, the "Entertainment Capital of the World;" and, of course, "The Pearl of the Pacific" – San Francisco.

San Francisco
San Francisco is one of the most attractive, enchanting and creative cities in the world. Few can match it for charm, class, culture and cuisine. As we depart for some faraway destination, I like to ask Tony, "Why are we leaving this magnificence; can any place offer more?" The truth is that we have never ceased to enjoy the surprising and unexpected gifts of the City by the Bay. Like the New Year's Eve midnight cruise underneath the Golden Gate Bridge when we saw a shooting star. Tony exclaimed, "That's an omen of good fortune. It's going to be a great year!" It was the first day of 1975. Three months later I was appointed cathedral rector and Tony Episcopal Vicar for Hispanics.

In recognition of Tony's work in the inner-city, Congresswoman Barbara Lee invited Tony to attend the inaugural of the new Martin Luther King Jr. Memorial in the nation's capital. Since I was in New York at the time, we agreed to meet in Washington for the weekend. Regrettably, the event was postponed due to the disruption of all air travel in and to the East Coast by Hurricane Irene.

I returned early and suggested that we celebrate surviving the ravages of the storm by having dinner in San Francisco at the Ritz-Carlton. In the lobby of the exclusive hotel off California Street I asked, "Have you been here before?" "Oh yes," replied Tony, "I came here with Pina Barbieri – in a limousine. You know, she always travels in a limousine – everywhere, even when she's in Europe."

Dr. Pina J. Barbieri was a pillar in Tony's parish. Her obituary referred to her as a "celebrated educator and businesswoman ... senior partner, corporate secretary and customer service manager of Richmond Sanitary Services." Her considerable wealth stemmed from prominence in the waste management industry. She was also a philanthropist who saw to it that her favorite pastor always had a little fund "to spend on the padres." Needless to say, dinner at the Ritz was on Pina! Nor would it be the last.

+++

I am not fond of Chinese food. Tony's tastes, on the other hand, know no boundaries. But both of us were introduced to the finest gourmet Chinese cuisine in Chinatown by visitors from Mexico. One day I received a phone call from the office of the archbishop of Tijuana. Could I arrange a tour of the San Francisco cathedral for the archbishop who was planning to build a new cathedral in Baja California? He was interested in finding out how San Francisco had proceeded in building the masterpiece called the "Chartres of the West."

Tony rented a Chevy van to pick up Archbishop Rafael Romo Muñoz and his entourage at their hotel on Market Street. In the group were a young priest secretary, a wealthy owner of a chain of stores in Mexico, and an architect who presumably would design the new church. (We were told that this same architect designed some of the sets for the movie "Titanic" which was partially filmed in Baja.)

We drove our guests to St. Mary's Cathedral on Geary and Gough where our friend the rector, Monsignor Jack "Bucky" O'Connor, greeted us and led us on an extensive and comprehensive tour of the complex. He also arranged for interviews with cathedral staff involved in the construction of the project. The Mexican prelate and his architect inspected the original blueprints while the merchant met with the people in charge of development and finance.

After the interviews our chain-store owner offered to treat us to dinner. Once in the van, the question of where to eat came up. The host said that he and his wife had a favorite restaurant but he couldn't recall the name. So, he dialed a number on his cell phone and asked, "What's the name of our favorite restaurant in San Francisco?" The voice from south of the border echoed, "Tommy Toy's in Chinatown!" *Bitte!* I mumbled from behind the steering wheel. Tony registered silent surprise with a hint of compassion – he knew my culinary aversions.

My initial reaction soon turned to amazement upon entering the famous eatery on Montgomery Street. An elegant hallway lined with photos of celebrity patrons blossomed into a jaw-dropping dining room. Tommy Toy's decor, we read "was fashioned after the 19th century quarters of the Empress Dowager's sitting room ... with three-hundred-year-old tapestries, hand silvered mirrors, powder paintings framed by sandalwood, etched glass panels, carved wooden archways, silk draperies, and Tommy's personal collection of original Chinese fans."

The cuisine and service matched the decor, as did the bottles of choice wines ordered with cosmopolitan gusto by our Mexican millionaire. After a private consultation with the maitre d', exquisitely prepared dishes streamed from the kitchen, which one might think was staffed with chefs trained in France: Seafood Bisque, Barbecued Duck Salad, Minced Squab, "Imperial" Satay Prawns, Pacific Sea Bass *en papillote*, Jasmine White Rice...

Tony's assessment: "Had I known that our little tour would conclude in such Oriental splendor, I would have raided Pina Barbieri's fund and rented a stretch limousine!"

Hollywood
One summer we decided to take a leisurely road trip – somewhere. We agreed to play it by ear one day at a time and see where we ended up. After breakfast, once in the car, I would ask, "left or right?" Tony kept saying "left." As a result, after overnights in Monterey and Santa Barbara we ended up at Universal Studios in Hollywood. We strolled through the exhibits and rides at the theme park, and rode

along soundstages and back lots featuring scenes from classic movies.

"Since we are in Hollywood," Tony insisted, "we should have dinner at one of those famous nightclubs." We made reservations and were informed that "coat and tie are required." Luckily, Universal City had a men's boutique with an impressive selection of blazers and cravats. I picked out a rather expensive combo, but then discovered that I had left my credit card at home. No problem: Tony would loan me the money. I conveniently forgot about the "loan" until a couple of years later when we were reviewing trips. Shame-faced I took him to Macy's in San Francisco and had him select a new sports coat – which I paid for with my "errant" credit card. At the time we had no way of knowing that our formal apparel would serve us well one day in the nation's capital.

Columbus' "new world discoveries" included many countries. We know some of them well. Our parents are from Mexico, where we have countless relatives. I lived there for three years as a student. Tony spent two years in El Salvador as a missionary. On a cruise to the Panama Canal we visited Costa Rica in Central America and Colombia in South America.

There are however parts of the new world "discovered" not by Spaniards but by Englishmen who explored the Pacific Islands. We were eager to check them out as well.

Chapter Twelve: Hawaiian Highlights

Our first journey to The Islands was a gift we gave ourselves for having successfully completed a master's degree program. Tony received his Master of Science in Counseling from California State University, East Bay; mine was a Master of Fine Arts in Electronic Music and Recording Media from Mills College, Oakland.

We traded academic robes for swimming trunks, and looked forward to testing the waves of the ocean and frolicking on hot and sandy beaches. This we did the very first day in Honolulu. After a few hours Tony misjudged a wave and twisted his foot. He feared he had broken two toes. I failed to keep hydrated and suffered an attack of sunstroke. The two of us hauled our battered bodies back to our hotel. This slight setback, however, was not going to keep us from having dinner that evening at Chez Michel!

Despite his aching toes, Tony agreed to walk across the park to the French bistro. We stopped in the middle of the spacious lawn area near a raised platform to rest. On the stage some Hawaiian performers were doing the Hula. Before one could say "Aloha," three lovely dancers, targeting spectators to join them on stage, zeroed in on Tony and friend. "We teach hula in one easy lesson." In front of a throng of tittering tourists they had us shuffling feet (ouch!) and swaying hips. I could see my partner grimace in pain, attempting heroically to smile at our undulating Polynesian instructors.

When we finally reached Chez Michel, all Tony wanted was a double shot of Jack Daniel's. This he repeated until he could no longer feel his toes. The bistro's interior was long and narrow with tables abutting each other. The arrangement made for an intimate environment when filled. The table-for-two next to ours sat empty for all of 10 minutes. As we began our salad the maître d' escorted two young women to the tiny table next to ours. We were seated so close that we might as well have been a party of four. The youthful twosome, eyeing us mysteriously, kept giggling and whispering knowingly.

For dessert we decided to splurge and ordered *Crêpes Suzette*. The waiter prepared the thin pancakes swimming in orange liqueur and cognac at the table. He torched the ingredients, creating a bonfire that raged dramatically until the cognac had evaporated. This took place right in front of the two startled girls whose eyes got as big as the crepes.

They looked so enthralled that Tony asked them if they would like to share some. No sooner had he issued his magnanimous invitation than the young lady closest to him leaned over and whispered, "I know who you are. You are FATHER Tony; and he is FATHER Don; and my aunt is Julie Bandau, your bishop's secretary!"

OK. Unmasked. Time to implement some diplomacy.

Since the bishop's secretary had been the one to forward the tuition checks for our graduate studies, it was our duty to return the favor by extending our FATHERLY attention to her unescorted niece and unescorted companion. So, we offered to chaperone both to the Top of the Needle for Don Ho's nightly show. As it turned out, we ended up rehearsing the Hula – broken toes and all – shuffling and swaying away. The lesson in the park, painful as it was for Tony, came in handy after all!

The next morning, we found a Kaiser Hospital where x-rays revealed that Tony's injury was not a fracture but a severe bruise - from which he recovered soon enough with a little more help from Jack Daniel's. Mahalo be to God.

Chapter Thirteen: Capital Capers

Washington D. C.

The day we arrived in our nation's capital for the first time, history was in the making. On May 17, 1973 Senator Sam J. Ervin was convening the Senate committee investigating President Richard Nixon's role in the Watergate scandal (the burglary at the Democratic National Headquarters). When we got to our hotel, Tony announced that he was going to the Capitol to witness the proceedings firsthand. I chose to view the event on television in the comfort of a hotel room. When Tony returned, he said that getting a taxi had been a problem – too many people going to the Senate. He was finally able to get a ride with several other passengers, all of them members of Congress.

While watching television I came across the entertainment channel giving the lineup of musical events at local theaters and clubs. Among the listing was the Ramsey Lewis Trio performing at the Bohemian Caverns at 8 p.m. While Jazz did not have the same effect on Tony as the music of a Wagner or Mozart opera, the popular piano renderings of the composer of "The 'In' Crowd" and "Hang On Sloopy" did hold a certain appeal. I suggested that we dress in our Universal Studio and Macy's jackets and ties for the occasion. "After all," I pointed out, "we are in the city of well-dressed diplomats."

Formally attired, we arrived at the Georgetown nightclub only to be told that the house was sold out. "I'm sorry, gentlemen," apologized the hostess at the door. "There are no more tables available, not even standing room."

Well, I'm going to have to do some creative maneuvering here.

Addressing Tony in Spanish, I relayed the information in a loud voice. In a lower tone, I instructed him to make a fuss and start remonstrating like an indignant Spaniard.

¡Vale, vale, pués hombre! ... (A low-key Latin version of the Munich routine ensued.)

I turned back to the concerned hostess, "Please forgive me for insisting. You see, I am the interpreter for the Ambassador of Venezuela. He was so looking forward to meeting Mr. Lewis and inviting him to his country. As you can see, *Señorita,* His Excellency is quite disappointed."

Before Tony could utter another *¡Vale, vale!* a waiter with a table hoisted over his head was escorting us to the foot of the stage and seating us directly in front of Ramsey Lewis' piano! Needless to say, the ambassador and his translator shamefully slipped away before the gig was over.

+++

We returned to the nation's capital 39 years later - 2012. It was at an equally historic time. Barack Obama, the first African American to be elected U. S. President, occupied the White House. He had selected the first Hispanic-American woman as Treasurer of the United States. It was her signature that appeared on every American paper currency – "Rosa Gumataotao Rios."

And "Rosie" Rios was a friend of Father Tony - now Monsignor Valdivia. Rosie's mother Guadalupe "raised all nine children on her own and with the support of her church sent all of her children to Catholic schools and on to college." (*Wikipedia*). The Rios family were parishioners of St. Clement Parish in Hayward when Tony was assigned there and where little Rosie Rios attended elementary school.

Treasurer Rios welcomed Tony with a warm *abrazo* and both of us with genuine delight. "It's such a pleasure to welcome friends from back home!" she repeated as she led us into the Treasury Building adjacent to the White House. On the way to her office she pointed out the room where President Abraham Lincoln first ordered paper currency to be printed in order to fund the Civil War. When we reached her private chambers, she dialed her phone and gleefully announced, *Mamá, ya llegó Monseñor!* "Monsignor is here!"

Ms. Rios then took us out onto the "Terrace" – just yards away from the East Wing of the White House. "Michelle Obama has her office right over there," she gestured. Our hostess went on to explain that she had been one of the two dozen members of Obama's financial transition team that met "here" during the financial crisis of 2008. "President George W. Bush used this entrance every day to come and advise the group," she observed.

Our distinguished guide then escorted us upstairs to "take a peek" at the suite of the Secretary of the Treasury, Timothy F. Geithner. There she informed us that she would have liked to personally take us to her "other workplace," the Bureau of Engraving and Printing (BEP), but she had business to attend to with the Secretary. "However," she said with great satisfaction, "I have arranged for the bureau's project manager to personally give you our special VIP tour."

Our VIP tour began with Kevin Nance, the BEP's young manager, welcoming us warmly on behalf of his boss. This was followed by a security screening in a private lounge where one is politely invited to secure (surrender) cell phones, pagers and recording devices. Thus unencumbered, Nance led us underground into the heavily guarded precincts where the nation's official paper currency is designed, printed and "sliced."

Regular tourists witness the process from windows on an upper floor; VIPs are ushered into the "factory" where the money is made. Acknowledging the presence of their boss, workers paused to explain to his guests their particular operation. One was an artist-engraver designing a new $100 bill; another specialized in mixing the authorized tint of green ink. A machine encoded each bill with a specific identity-number while paper sorters and monster printing presses disgorged sheets of greenbacks ready to be sliced into wallet-size banknotes.

At the end of the tour Nance placed in Tony's arms a "brick" of $100 bills. [A brick is a stack of unsliced currency, 30 by

30 inches long and 6 inches high, weighing 15 pounds.] "You are holding $100,000," he announced. At that, a nearby engraver chirped, "Have a nice day with that!"

As he walked us back to the exit, Kevin commented on how pleasant it was to entertain Treasurer Rios' Latino friends. "The last time we conducted a VIP tour like yours," he informed, "was for Carlos Slim from Mexico. At the moment, according to Forbes, Mr. Slim is the richest person in the world."

+++

While in D. C. we were further enriched by touring the many historical and cultural sites of the capital: The Holocaust Memorial Museum, Lincoln's Museum, Ford's Theatre, The National Museum of American History (Smithsonian), The Martin Luther King Jr. Memorial, The John F. Kennedy Center for the Performing Arts (featuring the Washington Ballet in *Noche Latina*). In previous trips we had visited the many presidential and war memorials as well as the White House and the Capitol with the Houses of Congress. But the visit with the Treasurer of the United States without a doubt yielded Tony and me the most bang for our bucks!

Chapter Fourteen: To Mexico With Love

We have been to Mexico more times than we can count. Our parents were born and raised there, immigrating to the U. S. at the end of the Mexican Revolution (1920's). Tony's folks came from the Lake Chapala region in the State of Jalisco where his father Juan ferried people and cargo from shore to shore. My Dad Jesus, a lieutenant *coronel* in Pancho Villa's revolutionary army, was forced to flee his native Sinaloa under threat of execution by dueling factions. Our Moms Cruz and Gaudencia also fled the rages of civil war, joining our Dads and settling in Oakland, California where Tony and I - the youngest of 8 and 10 siblings respectively - thrived in nurturing households.

Because our parents had many siblings who remained in Mexico both of us have more relatives there than we can count. Most of our trips down South have been visits to family. On those occasions we function as chaplains, presiding at cousins' weddings, baptizing their children, celebrating First Communions and *Quinceañeras*, hearing confessions, giving counsel, mediating feuds, blessing homes and vehicles, assisting the sick and dying - in short, performing in-house family ministry.

However, because we come from the United States - the land flowing with "milk and money" - our mothers insisted that we also be ministers of Made in America merchandise. So, before every departure our mamas would saddle us with suitcases stuffed with slacks and sweaters for the uncles, blouses, skirts and jewelry for the aunts, Keds, creams and cosmetics for the cousins – and don't forget the candy for the babies!

Although our respective relatives lived in different parts of the country, we did on occasion meet each other's clan members. I remember being introduced to Tony's matronly aunt Tia Angelina. She greeted us affably and immediately confiscated the suitcases that her sister Cruz had sent with Padre Tony. We learned later that the matriarch distributed the contents "judiciously," that is, only after determining who would get what based on the hierarchy of the tribe. After all, she claimed, Cruz had sent *las cremas* expressly at her request.

Tony remembers when we stayed at the home of my cousin Arminda in Guadalajara. At the time she was burdened with raising six live-wired children. Her husband, Cuco, was very hospitable; he kept shouting out, *Vieja, atienda a los padres!* "Old lady, take care of the Fathers!" We felt so sorry for the poor woman who would have to leave her brood or housework – or her slumber - scramble down the stairs, and cook up another meal or fetch another item at the whim of her solicitous slave driver.

Now one can understand why, along with presiding at happy and holy events, we had to now and then hear confessions, give counsel and mediate family feuds!

On occasion, Tony and I sailed off for Mexico without clerical collars or liturgical robes. Instead, we packed swimwear, sandals and summer casuals. Dressed as tourists we flew to the Mexican Riviera to relax and explore the beaches of this lovely land of the New World.

In the early 1970's the Mexican government began developing huge resort cities on the country's pristine and virgin shoreline along the Caribbean and Pacific Oceans. Eager to explore these ambitious developments we decided to check them out.

In Cancún we swam in the crystalline waters of the Caribbean, visited the nearby Mayan ruins and enjoyed the zesty music and cuisine of the Yucatán Peninsula. While the location was spectacular, the Cancún project had yet to develop adequate fun and entertaining activities - what tourists call "action."

Nor was there much happening at the newly installed resort city of Ixtapa next to the ancient and charming village of Zihuatanejo. The most fun we had there was at the sparkling Krystal Hotel - running into and taking our picture with Captain Charlie the chimp!

Not so in the more traditional resorts on the Pacific Coast. Acapulco was always alive with plenty of water sports and musical attractions – boating, water-skiing, *música Mariachi* and *danzas folklóricas.*

Plenty of action, too, in Puerto Vallarta which blossomed into a haven for vacationers after Elizabeth Taylor and Richard Burton exposed the enchantment of its scenic playground and tropical jungle - not to mention its colorful iguanas.

One year, Tony and I celebrated with seminary classmates our yearly reunion at Mismaloya, where *The Night of the Iguana* was filmed. We all had a pleasant week at the beach, except that no one warned us about the sand fleas. When these insects bite they deposit their eggs under a victim's skin. Upon our return to the States, both Tony and I had to run to a doctor - the baby fleas started hatching all over our itching bodies!

But the liveliest "action" occurred in Mazatlán, the rustic, care-free, let-your-hair-down, anything-goes resort located in the notorious State of Sinaloa. It is the kind of place where one can let go, release inhibitions, express pent-up frustration - in short, go wild. Which is exactly what happened at Señor Frog's.

Here's how it all came about. Tony had recruited three seminarians from Mexico as interns to assist him in the parish's Hispanic ministry. The arrangement was that they would provide pastoral assistance in exchange for room and board in his rectory. At the same time, our bishop who lived with me at the cathedral rectory invited his visiting nephew from Ireland to move in with us while in California. However, since his uncle was too busy to entertain him, it fell to me to "baby-sit" the 21-year-old Irish lad whom we christened "Pee-Jay" (P. J.)

Ever ready to assist me as well, Tony's three Mexican seminarians befriended P. J. showing him around town and introducing him to "Gringo" customs. It didn't take long for the trio to suggest: "Wouldn't it be nice if we could introduce P. J. to the beauty and culture of Mexico – maybe over Easter vacation?"

OK, we thought: We can make a quick jaunt to Mazatlán. Yellow light! Agreeing to chaperon four robust college-aged broncos on Spring Break is asking for trouble - no matter what vocational commitments they may be contemplating.

Mazatlán

The first thing the three Mexicans did was to introduce their Irish *amigo* to good old home-made Tequila. A bottle was purchased and passed around at the beach. Toasts to "*Mi amigo Pee Jay*" lasted until lunchtime. The self-proclaimed tour guides then led us to where the Gringos hang out – so that Pee Jay and the Chicano Padres would feel at home, "the most famous restaurant/bar in Mazatlán," Señor Frog's.

The happy quartet – with chaperons in tow - continued sampling the native beverages, this time the Margaritas. When the in-house Salsa band began serenading, the singing started, then the dancing – on the tables! That's when the manager confronted Tony and ordered him, "Rein in your horses or the police will be called!" The police were called. Tony instantly shifted into rescue mode, frantically hailing two taxis and corralling us like a seasoned wrangler into our get-away vehicles while approaching sirens blared and red lights flashed.

Yes, *Amigos*, we found plenty of action in Mazatlán! I'm happy to report that our three (chastened) Mexican seminarians, Francisco Javier, Guillermo and Pascual were all ordained priests in due course; P.J. we married off to a lovely lass from County Clare; and all of us learned a valuable lesson: Always stop at a yellow light – before things start turning red!

Update: "**Señor Frogs** has permanently **closed** and the space has reopened under a different name…" (Google).

"Ixtapa-Zihuatanejo"
Captain Charlie with two padres on holiday

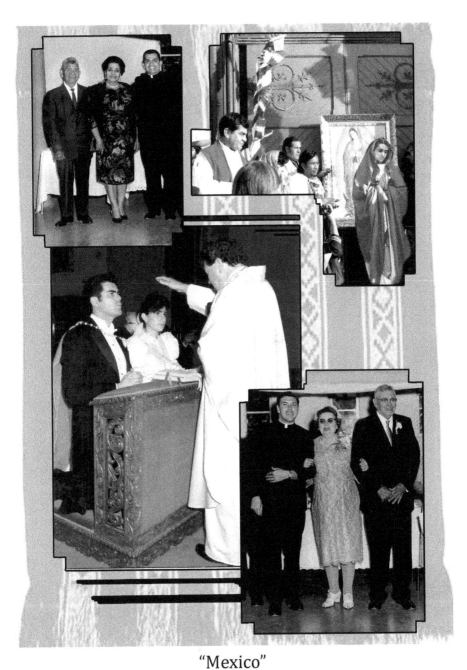

"Mexico"
(top) Juan and Cruz Valdivia w/son Tony; (center) Blessing
cousin's marriage; (bottom) Jesus and Gaudencia Osuna
w/son

PART III

Blending the New and the Ageless

Chapter Fifteen: Manhattan Prelude

Our grand tour of Italy and Sicily began and ended in New York City. For me it remains the favorite of our holiday experiences. I guess by then we had learned the secret to planning a successful vacation: Plan around people. Meeting friends and making new ones, that is what enhances, enriches and makes the journey worth remembering. Here are my journal entries for the beginning of our month-long memorable odyssey.

September 2. We landed at JFK Airport and made our way to America House, the Jesuit residency on West 56th Street in Midtown Manhattan. To my surprise I was given a remodeled room with double bed and TV. No such luck for Tony – he stayed in one of the dinky ones - *sans* amenities. After a chat with Charles Whelan, S.J., professor of law at Fordham, we enjoyed a lavish feast at Trattoria Dell'Arte, around the corner from Carnegie Hall – highly recommended by my brother Jess. Superbly Italian!

Tuesday 9/3. At breakfast Steve Pisano, S.J., professor of textual criticism at the Biblical Institute in Rome, filled us in on house rules and dining protocol. Thomas Reese, S.J., editor of America Magazine and author of "Inside the Vatican," shared the latest Roman gossip. A long walk to the Metropolitan Museum of Art awarded us with an exhibit of Gauguin's colorful scenes of Tahitian beauties.

At 4 p.m. Jess, sporting a freshly grown beard for a play he was in, joined us at Fox News. Annie Woolsey, an employee of the agency and whom I had baptized as an infant, led us on a tour of the studios, then via subway to Ground Zero where she was conducting interviews of survivors of the 9/11 attack on the World Trade Center. The experience was sobering -- stunning one into silence before the countless shrines to the fallen.

Jess suggested having dinner at Joe Allen's, a hangout of the Broadway stars and actors. Then he walked us over to the St. James Theater for a performance of "The Producers" starring Brad Oscar. The show was outrageous, irreverent and thoroughly entertaining.

Wednesday 9/4. Despite challenging and confusing rides on the NY subway, we made our way to the Battery Park Ferry for a tour of the Statue of Liberty and Ellis Island. Thanks to the excellent directions of the NYPD we arrived on time at the New Amsterdam Theatre for the matinee performance of "The Lion King" – dazzling, breathtaking staging that stretches the limits of creativity to new heights. Bravo! Dinner at Shelly's of New York, another one of Jess' favorite eateries. He ordered the filet mignon w/bacon/blue cheese, Tony the Chilean Sea Bass, and I a luscious salmon – simply "take a bow" cuisine!

Thursday 9/5. Our attempt to get to Santiago Calatrava's new digs via subway involved backtracking and wandering all over the underground system in oppressive heat. Upon arriving at 711 Park Avenue, Robertina Calatrava gave us a tour of their seven-level Victorian structure impressively remodeled in contemporary style and featuring Santiago's sculptures along with an inspired staircase that spiraled from basement to rooftop terrace. A date was set for us to bless the place when we returned from Italy. Back at our hotel a refreshing siesta strengthened us for the NFL Kickoff Concert featuring Bon Jovi and Enrique Iglesias in Times Square – with a crowd of thousands. Manhattan at its best!

Friday 9/6. I awoke early and walked to St. Patrick's Cathedral for 7:30 a.m. Mass celebrated by Cardinal Egan, recently appointed Archbishop of New York; then to Lincoln Center to purchase tickets for a New York Philharmonic performance upon our return trip from Europe. At noon Tony and I headed for JFK, then to Dulles airport in D.C. and lastly to Milan via United Airlines Business Class – the best way to relax and recoup after five exhilarating days in "The City That Never Sleeps."

Chapter Sixteen: Italy from Tip to Toe

The following 21 days were equally stimulating and eventful as we motored through Italy and Sicily. The van we rented in Milan took us from the northern province of the country (Piedmont) through the western regions of Liguria, Tuscany, Umbria and Lazio. In Rome we joined a Trafalgar bus-tour that transported us through Campania, Calabria and on a ferry across the Strait of Messina to the Island of Sicily. From Palermo we flew back to Rome, took the train to Milan where we boarded a return flight to New York City. Here's how it started.

Lake Como
It took us only one hour to drive from Milan to the Grand Hotel in Tremezzo and a 20-minute ferry ride to the isle of Bellagio on Lake Como. The scene was spectacular. Rain and thunder added Wagnerian drama to the geographic wonder of the Alpine peaks and foothills in the distance - highlighted by the setting sun.

On Sunday, we jet-ferried to the cathedral in Como, the largest village on the lake. Countless outcroppings of villas and residences nestled along the lakefront revealed centuries of summer entertainment for the rich and powerful as far back as the Caesars.

Monday morning, we set out for the Ligurian coastal highway. It's hard enough learning the rules of the road in a foreign country; it's an ordeal to contend with Italy's toll-road protocols.

On an *autostrada* one must stop at the toll-taking machine, insert a credit card, retrieve the card with receipt and move on. We come to the first toll station. To our dismay there are no human toll takers to speak to – all is automated. Tony hands me his credit card. I insert it. The machine says something in Italian and refuses to spit out Tony's credit card. Tony argues with the machine. This goes on for five minutes. The cars behind are honking hysterically. I move away. Tony gets hysterical, exits the van, runs back to the machine just as the motorist is about to retrieve a card that the machine is spitting out. Tony snatches the precious plastic and hysterically announces to the incredulous driver, *Questo è mio!* On to the next toll booth we go – prepared to battle mechanized monsters.

Santa Margherita
Things don't get any better when we arrive at the Hotel Continental in Santa Margherita. After leaving our belongings in the apartment, we took a side trip on a trolley to Portofino, one of the Jet-setting crowd's favorite hangouts. We enjoyed lunch in the central plaza that resembled a Broadway stage set.

Returning to the hotel, I'm the one who gets hysterical this time. My travel case is missing! It contains all our hotel vouchers, Trafalgar tour documents and return airline tickets! *Did the housekeepers steal the blue purse while we were in Portofino?* I was on my way to make a police report when Tony sheepishly remarks, "Oh here it is. I guess I put it in with my things. I thought it was my travel case. Sorry!"

We washed away all lingering anxiety in the hotel's unique swimming pool which was actually an inlet of the Mediterranean Sea. It felt like an Italian baptism.

Cinque Terre

Cinque Terre is a string of five centuries-old seaside villages on the rugged Italian Riviera that slope into the Ligurian Sea; which only proves that Italian skill can tame any terrain no matter how steep. At Riomaggiore, the farthest of the terraced wonders, we took a wrong turn and found ourselves wandering down plazas and alleyways reminiscent of Medieval times. At Vernazza we lunched at Gianni's which featured an antipasto of anchovies prepared in five different ways - some fresh, some aged in brine. We returned via train through Monterosso al Mare, ending up like the villages, in the sea at the hotel's delicious swimming hole.

Siena/Assisi

We were looking forward to meeting up with friends from the States who had rented a villa on the outskirts of Siena. The three widows were ecstatic when we drove up. "Thank God you've arrived!" they cheered, explaining that they had been "dumped" in the remote estate "without transport of any kind." The damsels were in physical distress as well: Colleen's knees were giving out, Evie had a painful rash (shingles, as it turned out), and Deedee had to play nurse.

To everyone's relief, we converted the Opel van into a comfortable three-seat "tour bus." Our first excursion was a pilgrimage to Saint Francis' hometown of Assisi. We were all enchanted by this holy village now fully restored after a devastating earthquake. Restored as well were the spirits of our ailing trio – after healing blessings in the chapel and a robust Umbrian meal with plenty of Tuscan wine.

The next day we "transported" ourselves to the center of Siena to view the Duomo with its extraordinary mosaic floors, which lucky for us, are on display only in the month of September. After a visit to the Shrine of Saint Catherine we delivered the ladies back to Casa Toscana where we celebrated a farewell meal, leaving the widows a little merrier. It was time for us to tackle the *autostrada* once again – this time to *Roma*.

Rome
We arrived at the Hotel Ripa in Rome by some miraculous angelic intervention. Despite his linguistic prowess, Tony was unable to decipher the directions to the hotel. All he could make out was its location: "somewhere in Trastevere." By some transcendent power I was inspired to exit the *autostrada* on instinct. I turned onto a main street and inserted the van behind a trolley. We couldn't believe it! The sign on the trolley read "Trastevere!" We followed it to our desired destination.

Once registered at the hotel, our next task was to return the vehicle to Hertz. I was not about to venture again into that Roman frenzy without expert guidance. Receiving another inspiration, I instructed Tony to summon a taxi and tell the driver he wanted to go to Hertz rentals in

Vatican City. I followed the taxi to our desired destination. On the way back, Tony was struck by a divine suggestion: "Let's pick up a bottle of gin and some Hennessy brandy." Bravo, bravissimo!

+++

Trafalgar Tour
At 7 a.m. on Sunday, Sept. 15, we met Anna, our energetic and enthusiastic Trafalgar tour-guide who always called us to attention by saying, "*Allora,* my people!" She introduced the 46 fellow tour mates, mostly married couples from English-speaking countries, identifying Tony and me as "two gentlemen from San Francisco."

Capri
Napoli was the springboard for the first highlight of the tour: The Isle of Capri, a spectacular island paradise in the middle of the Tyrrhenian Sea. Some of us opted to make the landing by boarding the small craft that hugged the island's rugged coastline. We were treated to a splashing adventure though monumental arches and fearsome caves thriving with scuba divers. Tony who had propped himself precariously in the front of the raft to "get the best view" was rewarded with a thorough drenching.

Once on land, minibuses transported us upward on the soaring rock to a scenic restaurant in Anacapri overlooking the entire Campanian coast – from Napoli to Amalfi. Lunch was followed by a walk through the town square and villas built into the face of the hill with wide-angle vistas of enchanting landscapes. Finally, we were bused to our hotel, the Regina Cristina, in the "molto very posh" district of Capri. Nowhere have I seen such elegant shops and boutiques. There is even an Andrea Pfister shoe store - with footwear starting at $500! No wonder this is a haven for the jet set.

The return ferry took us to Sorrento on the mainland where we boarded a luxury motor coach bound for the "Toe of Italy." We cruised in comfort past Salerno, Monte Cassino and the length of Calabria, a region rich in fruit and olive trees, all kinds of produce and cheeses. When we arrived at the mainland's southernmost harbor a huge ship docked in the marina was waiting to ferry us, bus and all, across the Strait of Messina to the storied island of Sicily.

Chapter Seventeen: Slices of Sicily

Taormina
While I rested at the hotel, Tony took the optional morning excursion to Mount Etna, a 10,912 ft volcano that over the centuries has caused so much destruction and death in the region – and would erupt again days after our departure! In the afternoon we joined the group for a visit to the Greek amphitheater in Taormina. Like all of Sicily, this ancient site features remnants of the island's numerous occupiers: Phoenicians, Carthaginians, Greeks, Romans, Vandals, Ostrogoths, Byzantines, Islam, Normans and Spaniards. The influences of these various civilizations are reflected in the country's multi-layered culture as well as in its "inclusive" cuisine.

As we motored south, Mount Etna loomed in the foreground crowned with a cirrus cloud resembling a landing UFO. "*Allora*, My People," Anna intoned, "Mount Etna is wearing her 'Contessa Hat.' She always does that to let us know that winter is approaching. Time to buy lots of warm sweaters in Sicily."

Siracusa (Syracuse)
In Siracusa we were taken to another Greek amphitheater. This one features the "Ear of Dionysius," an uncanny acoustical cavern that perfectly echoes what is spoken on the distant stage. The local guide, a witty English matron named Wendy, entertained with a lecture on the origin and nature of Greek Tragedy. The word, she said, is derived from "tragos" meaning black goat. Every year a *tragos*

was sacrificed to Apollo during festivities that featured theatrical productions; hence the term "tragedy." On this very site, Wendy added, "Euripides premiered his *Medea* to disappointing critical reviews."

As in the arts, Siracusa is notable as a city of the sciences. It was here that Archimedes, the Greek mathematician, physicist, engineer, inventor and astronomer, created his ingenious principles of physics, notably the displacement of water: weight equals volume. On the occasion of his discovery he uttered his famous "Eureka!"

Moving on to the center of town, we visited the duomo that was originally a temple dedicated to Athena. It was later converted into a church by Catholics and Byzantines and then into a mosque by Arabs. The ancient Doric columns still document its Hellenic origin.

Countryside
The long drive through the fertile Sicilian countryside called the "bread basket of Greater Greece" revealed miles and miles of wheat fields, olive and almond groves and acres of "dwarfed" vineyards. We made a brief stop at Villa del Casale, a fourth-century Roman mansion. Everyone was astonished at the remarkable mosaic floors depicting mythic tales from pagan literature – masterpieces of craftsmanship and artistry. As we approached Agrigento, we were equally amazed at the Valley of the Temples with restored shrines to Hera (Juno) and Hercules among others. Lunch on the beautiful beach at San Leone and a refreshing toe-dipping in the Sea of Africa reenergized our tired limbs.

Èrice (airy-chay)

No one prepared us for the wonder that is Erice! It's as if the gods had plunked down a mountain in the shape of a wedding cake and placed on its peak a jeweled crown. To reach this soaring aerie in the sky our motor coach had to wind its way upward for 2,460 feet, hugging the face of the rock and caressing ever steeper precipices. When it reached the vista point just below the fortressed crown, we disembarked and gasped. Half of Sicily and the Tyrrhenian Sea, it seemed, lay at our feet!

"Allora, My People, you have the rest of the day to explore on your own this stunning slice of Sicily." Tony and I discovered the ancient shrine first dedicated to Aphrodite by the Greeks, then to Venus by the Romans and by subsequent civilizations to their own versions of love-goddesses. As we wandered through the enchanted alleyways we chanced upon Ristorante Monte San Giuliano, an eatery at the top of the world featuring a menu of heavenly delights. The most memorable meal of the Italian sojourn awaited us inside. The solicitous waiter guided us through an authentic Sicilian meal: antipasti, primo, secondo e contorno (couscous drizzled with fish broth *a la Arabe*), insalata, formaggio e frutta, and dolce – a transcendent cannoli that transported Tony into Dante's *Paradiso.*

Palermo

The descent from unforgettable Erice leveled out onto the coastal highway along Castellammare del Golfo, past the island of Isola delle Femmine and ended at Astoria Palace Hotel in Palermo, the congested capital of Sicily. In the center of town is a marketplace unlike any other: blocks of stalls and shops overflowing with fresh fish, meats, vegetables, clothing, household furnishings, hardware, jewelry and any other item one can need or want.

The duomo dates from the eleventh century. It is influenced by Arabic architecture which the tolerant Norman invaders blended with the Romanesque to create a unique style. Embedded in one of the exterior columns is a page from the Qur'an. Inside are the tombs of four Norman Kings, including that of Ferdinand II "Stupor Mundi" (wonder of the world) who spoke several languages and instituted a democratic form of government.

For both Tony and me, the most impressive site in the Sicilian capital was Monreale, a stunning cathedral built by William the Good who created a second archbishopric in order to counter the power-hungry archbishop of Palermo. The edifice is a masterful blend of Byzantine-Roman-Arabic art. Its naves and sanctuaries glow with wall-to-wall 24-karat gold-plated mosaics depicting biblical scenes from the Old and New Testaments.

Without a doubt, Monreale reflects and embodies the artistic legacy of the civilizations that over centuries created the cultural mix that makes this island so unique. It was the perfect conclusion to our tour which Anna-*Allora*-My-People labeled "The Best of Sicily."

Chapter Eighteen: Roman Reprise

In Rome we rendezvoused with two former parishioners: Maureen, a retired corporate assistant, and Karen, a retired special education teacher. Both were visiting the Eternal City for the first time. It was going to be fun for Tony and me to show them around. However, Karen, who makes friends with everyone, had done so instantly upon arrival. In the hotel lobby she struck up a conversation with Fabianne. Before she knew it, her young architect friend was insisting on showing Karen and her companions the "real soul" of her native Roma.

On Sunday morning our hostess-guide drove us to the Janiculum, a hill with one of the best scenic views of central Rome with its domes and bell towers. We strolled along the promenade, taking in the panoramic view of the metropolis below. We also enjoyed watching a puppet show with a squad of squealing Italian tots.

From there we made a pilgrimage to nearby San Pietro in Montorio where St. Peter was believed to have been martyred on a cross upside-down. We attended Mass and soberly contemplated the fate of the first bishop of Rome. The thought occurred to me: *The Roman Catholic Church was turned upside-down at the time of the Great Schism (1054) and during the Protestant Reformation. Could it happen again?*

After the service Fabianne treated us to a tasty pizza lunch in a local park then drove us back to the hotel to rest and prepare for supper at her parents' home.

At 8 p.m. Mario and Marco, Fabianne's architect colleagues, picked us up in two tiny Fiats and weaved through fierce traffic to an elegant condo in a residential suburb north of Rome. Fabianne's Lebanese mother Amal greeted us in perfect English. Her father Attilo, a lawyer and business executive, welcomed us with patrician grace and a glass of vintage Pinot Grigio.

Toasts were exchanged on the terrace overlooking tree-lined gardens. On a table, a spread of Mediterranean and Middle Eastern delights rivaled the side dishes in Erice. The conversation was wide-ranging and cheerful. Tony added to the entertainment by telling tales of our recent "occupation" of Sicily. At some point, I asked the three budding architects if they were acquainted with the works of Santiago Calatrava. Their answer was immediate: "Who isn't? He's the Leonardo da Vinci of our generation." Modesty prevented me from mentioning that the reincarnated da Vinci had invited Tony and me to bless his new offices on our return to New York.

Back at the hotel we all agreed that the entire day had been a rare gift from the Roman household gods. How fortunate and blessed we had been! All harbored the same thought: *How many tourists are befriended by a family and invited inside its world to savor slices of its country, culture and customs?*

+++.

The Vatican
Tony took over the role of Vatican tour guide. He had visited Vatican City on several occasions with our bishop

and knew the ins and outs of the Holy City. "Today," he announced, "we will explore St. Peter's Basilica from cellar to attic."

Archeological excavations underneath the basilica uncovered the original burial site of St. Peter. His tomb was on display in the area called "Scavi" in the ancient necropolis dating to the time of Constantine. One must descend several meters to reach the shrine. After we paid our respects to the rock upon which Jesus chose to build his church, we exited and continued our tour of the main level.

The interior of St. Peter's Basilica is a monumental space holding 6,000 worshippers. Architects tell us that on TV it doesn't look that big because the scale of the design is so perfect (*Grazie*, Fabianne, Mario, Marco). It took Maureen and Karen several subsequent visits to take in all the grandeur and to examine all the art. But on this day our guide was determined to show us the Cupola atop the basilica's dome.

So up we went to the roof of St. Peter's by way of lift and 320 steps. From that vantage point we surveyed the seven hills of Rome and the valley beyond. Standing alongside us towered the giant statues of the 12 Apostles to our right and left. We were in good company. We felt quite blessed.

We had the same feeling the next day in St. Peter's Square when Pope John Paul II was chauffeured through the crowd of thousands at the weekly general audience. As soon as Tony spied the white Popemobile heading our way, he signaled to Maureen and Karen to follow him. He stopped at what he knew was a strategic intersection and warned, "Get the cameras ready!" Sure enough: The Roman Pontiff, looking surprisingly fit and in good spirits despite his fragile health, passed right in front of us – within six feet. Karen swore that he looked at her and waved a personal blessing. Maureen countered, "It was for us all!"

Trastevere

For our final excursion we chose to introduce Maureen and Karen to Trastevere, the historic district across the Tiber. First stop was Piazza Santa Maria and the Church of Our Lady, one of the oldest and most charming shrines in Europe. The ancient chapel was all lit up and filled with singing members of the Sant'Egidio community.

Next was our customary visit with Ivano Langella the jeweler, a young artist/craftsman who fashions stunning creations in gold, silver, bronze and pewter. Susanna, Ivano's English-speaking girlfriend happened to be in the shop. She facilitated what turned into a shopping spree. We purchased broaches, pendants, bracelets and a jeweled cross. Ivano was so grateful that he escorted us to "the best restaurant in Trastevere," Checco er Carettiere on Via Benedetta. He delivered us into the care of the maître d' and ordered him to serve us a vintage wine from Lazio. Dante's *Paradiso* revisited!

Our delightful evening in Trastevere brought to a close our odyssey through Italy, tip to toe and Sicily, too. Like a gem, the experience reflected all the highlights of the entire trip. The name itself means "on the other side of the water." Having crossed an ocean, we rendezvoused with friends and made new ones who revealed and shared the magnificent landscape and magnanimous heart of the country. It was now time to once again cross over to the other side of the water and reconnect with our own people and home turf – for there was much to enjoy over there as well - and commitments to fulfill.

Chapter Nineteen: Manhattan Encore

In New York we resumed our cultural and musical agenda with a vengeance. First on the list: a concert at Avery Fisher Hall with Andre Previn conducting the New York Philharmonic in Haydn's Symphony #102, Ravel's Piano Concerto in G Major with soloist Jean-Yves Thibaudet, concluding with Shostakovich's Sixth. The wide-ranging program provided Tony and me the perfect medium to reflect and recall the myriad experiences of the past three and a half weeks.

During the entire second movement of the Ravel, a hauntingly beautiful Adagio for solo piano, an elderly lady in obvious distress was slowly escorted down the aisle and out of the hall. For me, the scene became a meditation and commentary on how advancing age sadly lessens one's ability to travel at will. For Tony who had his eyes shut, the score made him relive "the magic and mystery of Erice."

After dinner, we headed to the Metropolitan Opera in Lincoln Center for Zeffirelli's production of Puccini's Turandot. The staging was kaleidoscopic and the singing engulfing. However, by the second act, the onset of jet lag rendered both of us semiconscious, dissolving images and sound into a psychedelic dream sequence.

The next day we were totally sobered by the Met's production of Richard Strauss' Elecktra with Deborah Polaski in the leading role and Marjana Lipovšek as Clytemnestra. It helped that the performance was a matinee, allowing one to stay awake. The Greek-inspired psychodrama depicting the rage of two neurotic women with murderous designs was emotionally draining but musically gripping.

The theatrics continued that evening with Rossini's La Cenerentola featuring the young tenor from Peru Juan Diego Flórez who received two extended ovations for his sensational performance as Don Ramiro, hurtling volleys of high C's all over the stage.

Three operas and one symphony concert in two days must be some kind of record!

The cultural banquet climaxed with an elegant brunch at Calatrava's home and new offices on Park Avenue. It was preceded by a solemn blessing of the premises. I splashed Holy Water on the freshly painted walls of the seven-story edifice as Santiago, Robertina, Michael and Sophia led us from floor to floor. The whole while, Tony, belting out psalms, hymns and Spanish cantos, filled the space with sacred sound - matching any tenor at the Met. On the top floor the scene turned theatrical when brother Jess suddenly emerged from the stairwell panting. He had scrambled up seven flights of stairs, emoting apologies for arriving late.

The New York headquarters of Santiago Calatrava Architects and Engineers was officially blessed. But as Maureen said in Rome, it was a blessing "for us all." In this case it was a blessing for all the world. For from those offices sprang the designs for, among many others, the

Saint Nicholas National Shrine and the Transportation Hub at New York's World Trade Center.

That's the way the thirty days of September ended for two padres on holiday in the year of Our Lord Two Thousand and Yesterday – blessing and forever blessed.

Chapter Twenty: All Aboard for Russia

We finally made it to Russia twenty years after Chernobyl. We now know that plenty happened in Kiev despite the protestations of *Intourist*. Anyway, Kiev was no longer part of Russia; it became the capital of Ukraine. So, we bypassed it altogether.

We started our adventure in Saint Petersburg. After the breakup of the Soviet Union, the new Russian Federation opened its historic doors to a flood of tourists eager to explore the fabled treasures of the Czars. The summer residences of Peter the Great and Catherine the Great are more than spectacular - they are awe-inspiring. And the Hermitage Museum is even more breathtaking. One can scarcely imagine the opulence of the former empire.

The fact that it is the largest country in the world became evident as we traveled along its waterways on the Viking cruise ship Pakhomov. It took six days to reach Moscow. Each day we disembarked to explore a different site, settlement or city. Lakes, rivers, canals - and eighteen locks - revealed the vastness of the land and the multicultural nature of its inhabitants.

Since most of the time was spent onboard the ship, we enjoyed learning about the history and evolution of the Russian experience at daily lectures. One Russian speaker outlined the loss of national stability, universal government subsidy and the recent rise of capitalists and oligarchs. "Some of us feel," she declared openly, "that we were better off as citizens of the Soviet Union. At least under Communism everyone was equally poor!"

Tony had a field day talking to everyone. He introduced me to three couples from Mexico whom he had met on deck. We became friends and shared stories. On Saturday evening Tony mentioned that Juan, the businessman from Ciudad Obregon, had asked him ¿Y Usted en que trabaja? "What is your line of work?" "Did you tell him?" I asked. Before he could answer, an announcement over the loud speaker echoed through the entire ship: "Attention, this is your steward. Tomorrow morning at nine o'clock FATHER Antonio will be saying Mass in the lounge - adjacent to the bar. All are welcome."

From then on, the two bachelors from San Francisco were referred to as the "two padres on holiday." That evening at Talent Night Tony and I performed our repertoire from La Barca, including *Cucurrucucu Paloma* and "I Left My Heart in San Francisco."

From Moscow we flew to Prague in the Czech Republic, and from there to Portugal where we added to the list of pilgrimages to holy shrines.

"Ephesus"
Exploring the ruins of Ephesus in Asia Minor

PART IV

Sites of Grace and Insight

Chapter Twenty-One: Shameless Pilgrims on El Camino

According to our trusty travel agent Judy, Cascais on the Portuguese Riviera would be the perfect spot to relax before returning to the States. Our resort had a swimming pool where we leisurely planned each day's activities. Our first was a one-day pilgrimage to Fatima, a nearby shrine where the Blessed Virgin Mary appeared to three peasant children in 1917. The devotion promoting the recitation of the Rosary had spread widely and was very popular in our parishes.

To get to Fatima involved taking public transportation into Lisbon, then a train to the town of Fatima. But to get to the shrine which was several miles away, we had to hire a taxi. The return trip proved to be a problem – and a boon. After a prayerful visit to the basilica with the venerated statue of Our Lady, we discovered that no taxis back to the train station were available. We inquired at the local hotel about alternate transportation. The concierge was kind enough to phone for a car that showed up almost instantly.

A young man by the name of Norberto was behind the wheel of a new blue Astoria. For a reasonable fee he offered to take us all the way back to Cascais. On the way Norberto explained that he and his father were licensed tour guides; their specialty was driving pilgrims to and from any religious shrine in Europe.

Back in the hotel swimming pool, Tony said to me rather nonchalantly, "Do you think Norberto might be available to take us to Santiago de Compostela tomorrow?" Nonplussed, I replied, "Are you serious? It's 300 miles away – in Spain!" Tony mused: "To have come this far and not visit the most famous shrine in Europe would be a shame. Why don't you phone him and find out?"

I dialed the number on the card Norberto had left with us. The young man listened to my inquiry, asked his father if a vehicle was available and responded, "Sure, we can do that." Tony signaled to ask him how much it would cost. I winced at the answer and relayed the amount: 800 Euros. Tony signaled "thumbs up." A car would pick us up at 8 a.m. Continuing his nonchalance, Tony smiled and declared, "Pina will pay for it."

We were waiting in front of the hotel at the appointed hour. In the distance we saw a vehicle turning the corner with Norberto behind the wheel. He was driving a blue Mercedes Benz LIMOUSINE! Both of us were aghast. "See, I told you," Tony muttered triumphantly, "Pina Barbieri would take care of it. Obviously, she approves!"

The five-hour ride through the Sierra mountain ranges of Portugal got us to The Cathedral of St. James of Compostela. Pilgrims were arriving on foot, on bikes, in vans and even in wheelchairs. For weeks they had been traveling on "El Camino" enduring the hardships of road, weather and aching limbs. These two padres on holiday, on the other hand, had arrived in a chauffeured limousine. Shame, shame, shame! Nevertheless, we shamelessly joined them in approaching the statue of St. James the Greater at the high altar and, as is the custom of grateful pilgrims, touch the back of his head. When I bent over to look at his face, I swear I detected a twinkle in the eye and a hint of a smile.

Instead of returning by the same mountain route Norberto drove us home by way of Portugal's Atlantic coastline – as picturesque and scenic as Highway 1 in California. We arrived in Cascais at midnight. Thus ended the 16-hour trek of two shameless pilgrims on El Camino.

Chapter Twenty-Two: Egyptian Escapade

It was on Tony's Bucket List. So, the first place we had to visit when we got to Cairo was Mount Sinai – a seven-hour drive through the desert. Thanks to Judy our travel agent, a private van with two drivers and a personal guide were waiting outside our hotel at 6 a.m. It was so dark that we failed to notice the three Giza pyramids across from our hotel.

Our guide Adam was a Christian Coptic who was fasting (it was Orthodox Lent) and had a horrible cold. He was garrulous and fluent in English. He had spent time in Canada he told us, "because a Christian can't get a job in Egypt." We felt sorry for the poor chap who, when we stopped for lunch, went off by himself, sneezing and coughing – and famished. Taking turns, the two drivers headed north, sped through a long tunnel underneath the Suez Canal, then turned eastward along the length of the Sinai Peninsula to the city of St. Catherine at the foot of "Mount Moses."

It was our intention to climb to the summit. We had two options: the "Camel Path," which would take three to four hours on foot, or the steeper but shorter route requiring one to climb 3,750 steps called the "Penance Path."

We opted for the Camel Path. Mistake. Unless you were *on* a camel – which we were not about to do – you do not want to walk *behind* one. Camels, like all beasts, have no qualms of dumping their dung wherever they roam. It was quite a dance, trying to sidestep all those piles of "camel calling cards." We made a valiant effort but after an hour or so we descended to base camp and explored the sixth-century Saint Catherine's Monastery "with the world's oldest operating library."

We were told by a camel-riding Brit who made it to the top where Moses received the Ten Commandments that the sunset had been "simply biblical!"

As we drove back to Cairo – all of us now sneezing and coughing – I said to Tony, "I hope we have better luck with the next item on the Bucket List."

Chapter Twenty-Three: Mary's House

The Virgin Mary can be said to have many "homes" around the world: Lourdes in France, Fatima in Portugal; in Mexico the Basilica of Our Lady of Guadalupe, still others in Poland, Ireland, Italy, Russia. Practically in every country there is a shrine or chapel where the Mother of Jesus is venerated. In our travels we have visited several of them, but none as unique as "The Virgin Mary's House" in Turkey.

What makes it unique is its location. Not only is it in a country where Christians are a minority, but it is tucked away in a densely wooded area in the mountains outside of Ephesus. The remoteness and park-like setting enhance the charm of the modest dwelling where the mother of Jesus is said to have spent her last years.

Ahmed, our Muslim guide, picked us up on Sunday morning and drove us through pine forests to the entrance of the shrine. He remained in the car while Tony and I wandered off on our own in separate directions. As I came close to the smallest of the two principal structures, I heard a soprano voice chanting the Easter hymn *Regina caeli laetare Alleluia!* "Queen of heaven, rejoice." I instinctively joined in the singing: *Quia quem meruisti portare...* "Because the one you bore is risen..."

The soprano turned out to be one of the two nuns in charge of the shrine. She was taken aback that a tourist knew the Latin hymn. "Sister, I'm a priest," I informed her. "From where?" she asked. "From San Francisco." "How interesting!" she replied, "Sister Antonia is from San Francisco!"

As if on cue, Sister Antonia strode in with Tony in tow. "Look who I found!" she chirped, "A priest from San Francisco – and we share the same name!" After exchanging news from the States and about our respective parishes, Sister Antonia declared, "Both of you must stay for Mass at 10 a.m. A busload of pilgrims from Ireland will be here, so it will be in English."

I went back to the car to see if Ahmed would mind waiting a while longer. No problem; he would enjoy time with fellow guides drinking Turkish coffee.

Mass was celebrated out in the open on a platform under a canopy of fragrant trees amid glorious spring vegetation and a sea of Easter lilies. For me, this particular Eucharist at this unique place turned out to be the spiritual climax to a memorable Holy Week spent in Seville. It wasn't until we were in the car on our way to the airport that I realized the date – March 30, the 45th anniversary of my ordination to the priesthood. *Regina caeli...Ora pro nobis Deum, Alleluia!*

Chapter Twenty-Four: *Semana Santa en Sevilla*

Only the soul of Spain could render the Passion and Death of Christ refined and heartbreakingly elegant

Two decades after our initial "gypsy taste" of Seville, we returned for a more sober savoring: the city's celebrated ceremonials of Holy Week. We arrived by taxi on Tuesday. Processions were already blocking intersections around the cathedral plaza. Our driver dropped us off as close as he could, pointed in the direction of our hotel and told us to fend for ourselves. Suitcases in hand we weaved through a throng of spectators as a cortege of *Penitentes* approached *Catedral de Santa María de la Sede.*

To our immense surprise, delight and fortune, our travel agent Judy had booked us in *Hotel Doña María* – right in the cathedral's backyard! From the fourth-floor roof-terrace we could gaze down upon the *cofradías* (associations) entering and exiting the world's largest Gothic cathedral –and the burial site of Christopher Columbus.

The weather was ideal; it was springtime. The season promised warmth and a regenerated Earth bubbling with new life. That dynamic was also reflected in the rituals of Holy Week that culminate in the Resurrection of Christ. But first came his Passion and Death and Burial. The Spanish rituals focus on the inherent pathos of Christ's suffering and the grief of his sorrowful Mother. Lenten penitence is a means to identify with this suffering as well as to express guilt and reparation for so tragic a drama.

143

In other words, the Spanish take sin as seriously as they do blood. Jesus gave his life to atone for the sins of humanity, they firmly believe. Humans therefore must own their part in the tragedy and repent for having caused it. That acknowledgment they enhance with costume, choreography and music. And their striking statement is staged with a most refined and heartbreaking elegance.

More than 50 organizations called *cofradías* prepare all year long for the few hours it takes to exhibit their expiation, and bear their venerated images of the suffering Christ and his Mother in solemn procession through the streets of the city to the cathedral. After prayers, musical interludes and a blessing, the penitential entourage exits the temple to make room for the next *cofradía*.

Each participating confraternity is made up of hundreds of *Penitentes* in dark flowing robes; some with tall pointed hoods. Men take turns carrying on their shoulders large floats bearing life-size statues of the suffering Jesus and tearful Mary. The floats are festooned with mountains of flowers and flaming tapers. Acolytes with swirling censers create billows of sweet-scented cumulus clouds. Marching bands both at the head and at the rear blare mournful tunes maintaining the cortege in rhythmic order.

The pageantry is exquisite theatre. It is also genuine religious devotion. The portrayal of Christ in his criminal trial and subsequent crucifixion reminded me of John the Evangelist's depiction of the event as the triumph of a king who faced his ordeal with regal dignity and resolve. Pontius Pilate ultimately acknowledged it: "Then, thou art a King?" One of the *cofradías* is named after its statue of Jesus in regal robe and crown of thorns resolutely dragging along on his own an enormous Cross. *Jesús del Gran Poder* - "Jesus of Power and Might."

+++

There were some less ponderous moments that lightened the gravity of the Holy Week experience in colorful and cosmopolitan Seville.

Tony was keen on getting the "best seats" for the cathedral services which were first come, first served. He would arrive early, place himself at the head of the line, and rush in when the doors were opened. The chairs he reserved were close to the action – right next to the choir. However, we found ourselves seated right in front of the choir's Alto Section.

The Alto Section consisted of seven broad-chested *damas* whose chests matched their unbridled volume. Despite all his efforts, the desperate choir director, an old cathedral *canónigo* ("monsignor") was unable to tame the wailing septet. The only sound capable of drowning it out was the gigantic organ in the world's third-largest cathedral. Sadly, this magnificent instrument went silent after the *Gloria* on Holy Thursday evening, not to be heard from again until the ringing of the bells at Holy Saturday's Vigil Service.

So, we were subjected to an *a cappella* choir whose baritones, tenors and sopranos were rendered muted by the overwhelming roar of the seven Amazonian altos. (Listening to them became my Lenten penance!)

But there was one someone who made a greater impression than the altos. He even compensated for their deafening effect. It was the person and the oratory of the Cardinal Archbishop of Seville, Carlos Amigo Vallejo, O.F.M. (Franciscan, of course). His Eminence was an imposing presence: tall, silver-haired, elegant, charismatic, affable and mesmerizing as a preacher. We heard him give four homilies that engraved themselves in one's memory. Tony has them stored in his computer brain and can retrieve each of them virtually word for word.

What impressed me most, besides his eloquent sermons, was his ease and friendly relationship with his people. His concern for them became evident on Easter morning. I got up early and wandered over to the cathedral. The Cardinal was already there at the main door. Despite the fact that he had presided at the midnight Holy Saturday Vigil that concluded at three in the morning, His Eminence was up at 8 o'clock on Easter Sunday, fresh and genial. He was there to greet the last *cofradía* called *El Resucitado,* the "Risen One." The Cardinal was its chaplain and considered it a duty and a pleasure to welcome it as a fitting conclusion to the festivities of *Semana Santa en Sevilla.*

Seville is deservedly renowned for its beautiful women. And they were on display all during Holy Week. Dressed in black with lace headdresses (*mantillas*) draped over a tower-comb they strutted about town on the arm of escorts in dark tailored suits. At the Good Friday service two handsome and stately matrons in their distinctive attire preceded the Cardinal in procession and took prominent seats in the sanctuary. Royalty, civic leaders – or just a touch of class?

What makes Holy Week in Seville so memorable? The same thing, I believe, that makes its national dance and animal-sport so unique: an in-your-face approach to life and death. Spaniards perform these foot-stomping and death-defying activities with pride verging on arrogance; and they boldly wrap them in flamboyant artistry. When these traits are transposed into religious ritual the result is a Holy Week to remember.

¡Vale,vale! is a term that punctuates a Spaniard's speech. Literally it means: "It's worth it, it's worth it!" The word *vale* can also signify "cost" as in *¿Cuanto vale?* "What's the price?" When applied to the realities of life and death the Iberian ethos responds: "Life and death are precious, and one must pay for them with dignity, resolve and beauty. Life and Death are worth what they cost." *¡Vale,vale!*

Chapter Twenty-Five: A Pilgrim's Pageant

Oberammergau

As students in Israel Tony and I had visited many of the places made holy by the presence of Jesus: Bethlehem, Nazareth, the Sea of Galilee, the River Jordan, Cana, Jericho, Bethany, Jerusalem. When in those sites, we were encouraged to visualize the events that transpired there. But no effort of ours could begin to compare with the dramatic representation of events in the life of Christ as the Passion Play staged every 10 years in the Bavarian village of Oberammergau.

To experience this six-hour dramatization of Jesus' last days is spiritually transformative. To begin with, the scale of the production is overwhelming. Two thousand villagers comprise the cast and crew, including actors, commentators, choir, musicians, producers, directors, stage and technical teams – all of them local inhabitants. Years are spent in preparation. The length and structure of the play contribute to its impact. Like a river current, the inner dynamic carries one along gently at first; gradually it seeps into the soul then plunges one into a sea of emotion. Drawn into the action, one becomes a participant in the drama. Like good theater – and liturgy – the production invites, captures, nourishes and challenges.

This involvement of the audience is intentional, as the program notes reveal:

> The Passion Play is a mirror of the present for cast and audience ... The ones loyal to Jesus at the time, the

women or the Councilman Nicodemus for example, are not simply figures from the past, but human beings no different from the people of today who have a sense of salvation through suffering. Likewise, every one of the enemies of Jesus could be one of us, the "I" I call myself: Judas, Peter, Caiaphas, every one of those who don't exactly act in a noble manner... Every member of the audience can serve as an unjust juror or a part of a screaming mob. (*Textbook Preface Passionsspiele Oberammergau 2000*)

This connection between play and reality became clearer at noontime. After the morning's three-hour six-act segment, the audience is given a two-hour break for lunch. When the intermission began Tony was nowhere to be found; he had disappeared. When I finally located him he said, "I just had to get away by myself and be alone for a while." He needed time to ground himself; he was so moved and carried away by the dramatic action. "I felt as if I was there," he asserted. "Well," I said, "we are here, and it's time for lunch."

Pilgrims were flocking to the many eateries in the Alpine hamlet – all staffed by locals. It was in one of them that I, - as Tony had - underwent an "epiphany." The hostess who greeted and led us to our table, to our astonishment, was the actress portraying Mary Magdalene in the play! Our waiter turned out to be John the Baptist. I saw the apostle Thomas in the kitchen, and the bartender pouring drafts of beer was none other than St. Peter. And I recognized the Roman Centurion and one of the Pharisees – they were manning the checkout counter.

It was then that I realized more forcefully than ever: As in Jesus' days, we all live in a world of sinners struggling to become saints. Like the apostles, we doubt, deny and betray our principles if not our God. We move among Herods and Pilates and High Priests to whom we pay taxes. We continue to be inspired by prophets only to see them put on trial and crucified. I asked myself: *What role are you playing? Are you one of the loyal disciples or one in a mob swayed by the rhetoric of those who call for blood?*

The remaining three hours and five acts suggested a lot more questions. But the powerful ending provided the definitive answer to all of them. Death shall not have the last word. Efforts to silence, suppress, torture and kill what is good and true are doomed to fail. What will triumph in the end is the power of Goodliness to transform the dread of death into the promise of Paradise. "O death, where is your victory? O death, where is your sting?" (I Corinthians 15:55)

The conflict between good and evil – which is what the Passion Play is all about - rages on in every age and in everyone's experience. Jesus' story is history's story, his journey our own. The drama is playing out today as it did yesterday and will tomorrow. It is heartening to be told – with such conviction, sincerity and faith - that the storied journey ends in a sunrise of glory.

The Passion Play is meant to convey hope as a "Play of Redemption." Its major focus is close to the Johannine theology, which neither dismisses nor ideologically explains human shortcomings, malice and suffering.

Instead, we are challenged to continue to hope for a "Life in abundance" despite these imperfections and malformations. In this manner an ordinary person can look up to the One who is Raised on the Cross and draw strength from him. *(Preface)*

Epilogue

Tony and I are now in our retirement years. Our whirlwind junkets, guided tours, adventures, excursions and inspiring pilgrimages are over. The five decades of vacationing together are a rosary of memories. Every now and then we recall the joyful, sorrowful and glorious mysteries it retells.

We are most grateful to God for all the blessings bestowed while exploring the litany of treasures in his earthly Creation, including those in England, France, Israel, Greece, Hungary, Austria, the "New World," New York, California, Washington, Hawaii, Mexico, Russia, Portugal, Egypt, Turkey, Spain and Germany. I hope you enjoyed tagging along with *Two Padres on Holiday*. God bless – ¡Vale, vale! Amen and Oh, Alleluia!

Acknowledgments

Getting this book off the ground took quite an effort. I am so indebted to my skillful crew for their expertise in preparing for lift-off: Jack Miffleton, navigator, who masterfully laid out in detail the direction, trajectory and destination of our flight; Jerry Rubino who designed the craft's exterior and whose photo-art enhances its interior; Jo Ann Schneider whose eagle eye scrutinized every inch of the flight plan for pinpoint accuracy; and Michele Jurich who, sharing the editorial cockpit, kept us on course and supervised an on-target landing. Needless to say, as Captain, I must answer for any glitch or disturbance. To the passengers in the cabin and all members of the tour, thanks for making the global cruise such a memorable holiday.

Paz y Alegría!

Addendum

A Toast to Father Antonio A. Valdivia
On the Occasion of His 40th Anniversary of
Ordination to the Priesthood
St. Catherine of Siena Catholic Church, Martinez,
California
July 28, 2003

When one little first-grader asked, "How old are you?" Father Tony looked down at the inquisitive creature, anchored his feet firmly on the ground, strengthened his sturdy frame - tower like - expanded his arms horizontally and proudly replied: "I am as old as the Golden Gate Bridge."

Like that monumental structure christened 66 years ago, Tony has weathered many a storm, is getting a bit rusty but is still hanging in there. And may I add: the toll keeps increasing!

How to describe this priest's forty-year span of ministry? One word would be "successful." He has been eminently effective wherever he has been assigned: Castro Valley, Oakland, Union City, Hayward, El Salvador, Fremont, Richmond, Martinez. Why? What is the secret of his success? It's simple: He has been willing to give to his God, his family, his friends and his flock all that he has: a big mind, a larger heart, an expansive soul and - as can be observed - in an expanding body.

Let's take a look at each of these generous qualities.

His big mind. Father Tony has the mind of an historian. He observes and registers every fact, event, experience and impression. These he stores in his computer brain where they are processed, cross-referenced and sorted into truths, insights and conclusions. The thing is, he doesn't keep this acquired knowledge and wisdom to himself. Like everything else, he shares it with everybody – generously and conscientiously - in the classroom, the confessional, the pulpit, the bedside, the office, the dining room, the street corner.

Secondly, his larger heart. Here resides the love, care and sympathy for which Father Tony is deservedly renowned. At one time or another everyone here has experienced this man's loving hug, double-kiss and the greatest expression of his embrace - the gift of his laughter which brightens every occasion and softens stress, heartache and grief.

Thirdly, his expansive soul. Here resides the spirituality of a seeker. God, the Virgin Mary, the Church, the Priesthood – these mysteries play and dance endlessly in this man's spirit, nourishing and stimulating him to delve into new realms of mind and heart. Father Tony's greatest quality is his catholicity: Everyone is welcomed, everything is to be accepted; hardships, disappointments and challenges are but shadows caused by clouds temporarily shading the sun that is forever shining somewhere. Can you believe that this dreamer wakes up singing? There is a new song ever stirring in his soul!

And all of this is wrapped in a body, one can say, that was "Made in Mexico." A few words about that expanding waistline. His wardrobe is XXL as in extra-extra-large so as to accommodate any kitchen's culinary creation. As a child and adolescent, Tony grew up in his mother's restaurants. So, for him food has become an anchor, a comfort zone and a point of reference. When reminiscing about our many travels together, for example, I remember the venues, he recalls the menus. Well, using culinary terms, I would compare Father Tony to a super burrito whose rich and zesty ingredients are all rolled into one big jumbo-size tortilla. What a treat! And what a contribution to American culture! That in a word, *mis amigos*, is our Padre Tony!

I was saving this final remark for your funeral eulogy, Tony. But just in case I don't get the chance to use it, I'll say it now. When people ask me to describe in a couple of words, "Who is Father Tony Valdivia?" I will merely inform them of his preferred beverage, the drink he always ordered when he was most himself and the draft that perfectly mirrored his personality – a "Cadillac Margarita."

Nothing ordinary for that man! No, it had to be top of the line, best of its kind. What makes a Margarita a Cadillac, you ask? It's what crowns the tequila and the lime juice amid the Triple Sec – a shot of Grand Marnier. Yes, it was a "grandness" that distinguished Father Tony Valdivia - his big mind, his larger heart, his expansive soul. These are the qualities that over a lifetime transformed a small boy from West Oakland into a Cadillac of a Catholic cleric!

E. D. Osuna

"Retirement"
Celebrating a half century of ministry and travel

CPSIA information can be obtained
at www.ICGtesting.com
Printed in the USA
FSHW020859071219
64855FS